Inheritance Ta

C000038696

BDO Stoy Hayward is one of the UK's fastest growing major accountancy firms. Part of the world's fifth largest international network, with more than 600 offices in over 100 countries, it offers a full range of services including Audit, Tax, Corporate Finance, Forensic Accounting and Business Restructuring.

Wendy Walton is a partner in BDO Stoy Hayward, where she specialises in providing tax advice to wealthy private individuals, with particular emphasis on trust structures, inheritance tax and international aspects. She is a Chartered Tax Adviser, a Certified Accountant and a member of the Society of Trust and Estate Practitioners. She has written and lectured extensively on various aspects of personal and international taxation. Wendy enjoys spending her leisure time with her family.

John Porteous is an executive board director of BDO Stoy Hayward Investment Management Limited and head of its Private Client Services division. A former chairman of the Society of Financial Advisers and past board member of the Institute of Financial Planning, John is both a Chartered and Certified Financial Planner. He is also a regular commentator on financial planning matters in both the trade and the national press.

Inheritance Tax & Wealth Planning

A BDO Stoy Hayward Guide

Wendy Walton & John Porteous

P

PROFILE BOOKS

First published in 2008 by
PROFILE BOOKS LTD
3A Exmouth House
Pine Street
Exmouth Market
London EC1R 0JH
www.profilebooks.com

Text expanded and revised from *Inheritance Tax Planning* by Wendy Walton,
previously published in Great Britain in 2004 by PROFILE BOOKS LTD

A CIP catalogue record for this book is available from the British Library.

ISBN 978 1 84668 096 0

Typeset in Galliard by MacGuru Ltd
info@macguru.org.uk

Printed in the UK by CPI Bookmarque, Croydon, CR0 4TD

Contents

Foreword

NO ONE LIKES PAYING TAX. This is especially true of inheritance tax – it is a tax on the wealth you have built up during your lifetime, on which you have probably already paid income tax or capital gains tax. Inheritance tax continues to be of concern as property prices rise, pushing many people above the current inheritance tax threshold.

Looking on the bright side, there are lots of valuable exemptions and reliefs available, which means that with proper planning your inheritance tax bill can be minimised. The most valuable exemption states that if you give something away during your lifetime, it is free from inheritance tax provided that you survive for at least seven years after the gift has been made. This requires planning ahead to achieve a sensible balance between minimising the tax for your family while still keeping a comfortable lifestyle for yourself.

However, people often shy away from planning for inheritance tax or writing a will, as facing up to the prospect of death can be very difficult. Another reason for reluctance as far as inheritance tax is concerned is that, although the tax is paid on your wealth, it is the people to whom you leave your assets who actually suffer the tax.

Wendy Walton and John Porteous have had many years' experience in advising people how to preserve their family wealth. In this book they outline the various planning opportunities you can take to ensure that your family will not have to pay unnecessary taxes. Above all, they demonstrate that giving inheritance tax a little thought now can save substantial amounts later on.

JEREMY NEWMAN
Managing Partner
BDO Stoy Hayward

Acknowledgements

I WOULD LIKE TO THANK many people for their help. Michael Fernandopulle and Frances Niven gave invaluable assistance in updating the information. Andrew Franklin at Profile Books, my publisher, was also invaluable. And I would like to thank Jane Vass, who helped enormously with getting the book into its final form.

Finally, thanks to Justin, my children Gemma and Alex and my parents for their continuous support and encouragement.

WENDY WALTON

I WOULD LIKE TO THANK my wife Liz and son Max for all their support, encouragement and love. Also, the efforts and contributions of Gina Deacon and David Knight have been most valued in getting this text into a workable form.

JOHN PORTEOUS

1

Introduction

INHERITANCE TAX (IHT) is a tax due on your death and on certain gifts you make during your lifetime. Many lifetime gifts are exempt from IHT if you survive seven years from the date of the gift – but you have to watch out for other tax implications when making gifts, such as capital gains tax.

IHT can be an expensive tax, and a proportion of the wealth that you have worked so hard to accumulate during your lifetime (and paid tax on!) will go to the government rather than your family. It can also trigger strong emotions, particularly if it requires your children to sell the family home in order to pay the tax.

It has often been said that IHT is a voluntary tax – but without careful planning this is unlikely to be the case. If your estate is worth more than £300,000 (for deaths during 2007/08), then tax at 40% will be due on the excess. With increasing property prices, this threshold can soon be met. On an estate of £500,000, tax of £80,000 is due. According to Tax Commission statistics there were only an estimated 6% of estates that suffered IHT in 2006/07. But in actual money terms that equates to an expected total IHT bill of £3.6 billion for 2007/08.

IHT is still a political hot potato and the recently announced proposals to double IHT exemptions for married couples and civil partners, together with earlier changes to IHT on trusts, mean that now is an ideal time to review your financial position and consider the planning opportunities available. Failure to do so could lead to disappointment in the future.

This book seeks to give you an introduction to IHT – and covers the kind of planning that you can do as well as highlighting the pitfalls you need to watch out for.

Some chapters focus on specialist areas such as pension planning and the role of insurance. This shows how important it is to look at your plans for reducing IHT in the context of your overall financial planning. And given the recent changes to the tax rules relating to trusts, an increasing number of people will need to look into using insurance and investment-based strategies to reduce their IHT liability.

But as trusts will still play a part in the passing on of wealth, space has also been given to discussing the important duties of trustees – especially in relation to investment management.

One of the first steps in IHT planning is to ensure that you have an up-to-date will. You also need to add up the value of your estate and look at your income and spending. You may wish to make some lifetime gifts or change the mix of your estate, so that some of the assets qualify for IHT exemptions. Alternatively, you may want to think about generation skipping and setting up a trust for your grandchildren.

But whatever you do, you should always make sure that

you leave yourself with enough money and assets to cover your lifestyle and to provide for possible expenses – such as nursing care – in the future. Before giving anything away, you should also make sure that by doing so you are not potentially disqualifying yourself from state funding of care. This is unlikely to be a problem if you are currently in good health and it is clear that you are giving away assets as part of an IHT planning exercise, and not deliberately disposing of wealth as a way of avoiding paying for care yourself. However, it would be wise to seek separate advice on this issue.

This book is written as a general guide, starting with the basics, such as the importance of making a will, and going on to more complex tax planning, such as the use of trusts. Wherever possible, we have used examples to help make the position clearer. However, this is not a book about dealing with death, bereavement counselling, or the legalities of drawing up a will. We hope it will help you plan your affairs so you can pay less – perhaps a great deal less – tax. Whatever your course of action, you should consider taking professional advice as there are many pitfalls for the unwary.

Since 5 December 2005, same-sex couples who register their partnership under the Civil Partnership Act have been treated in the same way as married couples for IHT purposes. Throughout this book, the term 'spouse' is used to refer both to married people and those in civil partnerships.

The information in this book is based on the law and HM Revenue & Customs (HMRC) practice as at 15 October 2007 and includes reference to the proposals announced in the Pre-Budget Report on 9 October 2007.

2

Getting to grips with the basics

'WHY SHOULD I CARE about inheritance tax?' or 'Why should I worry about making a will?' are questions we often hear.

Whether or not you worry about IHT is really your personal choice. At the end of the day, IHT is not actually suffered by you and doesn't affect your lifestyle. Instead, it restricts the amount you leave behind for your family (your 'estate', defined in the box on the next page).

Having said that, IHT is an expensive tax. There is a tax-free threshold (known as the 'nil-rate band', currently £300,000), but the rest of your estate is subject to tax at 40%, although there are various exemptions. You cannot get round this by giving everything away just before you die, because gifts in the seven years before death count as part of your estate for IHT purposes.

Note that the nil-rate band of £300,000 and the rate of 40% are current for the tax year 2007/08. The nil-rate band has also been set for 2008/09 and 2009/10 at £312,000 and £325,000 respectively.

The table on page 10 shows the tax due on various sizes of estate and the effective tax rate. As you can see, an estate of £500,000 could lose almost one-fifth of its value in tax. But

Calculating your 'estate'

Your estate is basically the total of all your assets less your liabilities, such as your mortgage and credit card balances.

What should you include in the calculation of your estate?

Family home
Household contents
Personal effects, i.e. jewellery etc.
Bank and building society accounts
Shares and other securities
Investments with National Savings & Investments
Pension fund lump sums
PEPs/ISAs
Life assurance
Holiday homes
Cars/boats
Money owed to you
Other assets
Your share of jointly owned assets

What can you deduct from the calculation of your estate?

Mortgage
Credit card debt
Car loans
Other money owed by you

it is not all doom and gloom. If the thought of a large part of your estate going to the taxman depresses you, do not despair. There are lots of reliefs and exemptions that are available – for example, gifts to a spouse are tax-free – and with careful planning the taxman's share of the cake can be substantially reduced.

When embarking on an IHT planning exercise, the first

Example: drawing up a capital statement

Mr and Mrs Badger have the following assets:

Assets and liabilities at current values

	Mr Badger £	Mrs Badger £
Assets		
Family home	375,000	–
Household contents and personal effects	22,000	–
Bank and building society accounts	45,000	16,000
Shares and securities	22,000	20,000
Investments with National Savings & Investments	–	–
Pension fund lump sums	80,000	–
Other financial assets e.g. PEPs/ISAs	12,000	–
Life assurance	120,000	–
Holiday home	180,000	–
Car	25,000	–
Other assets	8,000	–
Money owed to them	–	–
TOTAL ASSETS	889,000	36,000
Liabilities		
Mortgage (covered by separate life insurance cover)	180,000	–
Bank loans and/or overdraft	5,000	1,000
Credit cards	5,000	1,000
Hire purchase agreements	–	–
Other liabilities e.g. funeral expenses	3,500	3,500
TOTAL LIABILITIES	(193,500)	(5,500)
VALUE OF ESTATE	£695,500	£30,500

and Mrs Badger on page 11, your financial position may change on death; for example your mortgage may be repaid on your death if you have life insurance for it. Not everybody does and this depends on the type of mortgage you have taken out, so check with your bank or building society. Your life insurance policy may also be 'written into trust' so that the proceeds don't fall into your estate for IHT purposes – see Chapter 5 for more on insurance.

You also need to take into account the way in which your estate is distributed on death. For example, gifts to your spouse are tax-free, so if you leave all your assets to your husband or wife there will be no IHT liability on your death.

In the past, leaving everything to your spouse could mean wasting your nil-rate band unless you took steps to set up a 'nil-rate band discretionary trust' in your will (see Chapter 9 for more on trusts). But proposals put forward in the 2007 Pre-Budget Report mean that spouses can now effectively inherit any unused nil-rate band. The changes mean that from 9 October 2007, any part of the nil-rate band which was not used when the first spouse died can be transferred to the surviving spouse to be used when working out the tax bill on their death.

A claim to transfer an unused nil-rate band should be made on the death of the surviving spouse – if this is after 9 October 2007 – and not on the death of the first of the couple to die. So all widows, widowers and bereaved civil partners who die on or after 9 October 2007 will be able to make use of the transferable nil-rate band. The example opposite, calculating Mr and Mrs Badger's IHT liability, illustrates the position.

Example: estimated IHT position for Mr and Mrs Badger

Mr and Mrs Badger from the previous example have not undertaken any IHT planning. They have basic wills that leave all assets to the surviving spouse, and if no surviving spouse, to the children.

Mr Badger dies first and leaves all his assets to Mrs Badger. As the mortgage is covered by life insurance, he leaves Mrs Badger with assets of £889,000 minus debts of £13,500 – £875,500 in total. There is no IHT due at this stage because Mr Badger has left everything to his wife and none of his nil-rate band has been used. When Mrs Badger dies, the person administering her estate will be able to make a claim to transfer Mr Badger's 100% unused nil-rate band to Mrs Badger's estate. This doubles the nil-rate band available to Mrs Badger's estate.

On Mrs Badger's death, the IHT due will be as follows:

	£
Estate from Mr Badger	875,500
Mrs Badger's net assets	30,500
Total net assets	906,000
Less: nil-rate band	(300,000)
Less: transferred nil-rate band	(300,000)
Taxable estate	306,000
IHT at 40% on £306,000	£122,400

Although Mr Badger's estate was tax-free, it has pushed Mrs Badger into the IHT bracket. However, because 100% of Mr Badger's unused nil-rate band is available to Mrs Badger's estate, the IHT bill is £120,000 lower than it would have been without the transferred nil-rate band.

Writing a will

The most important aspect of IHT planning is writing a will but just as important is making sure that you keep your will up to date. The changes contained in the Finance Act 2006 to the way IHT is charged on trusts (covered in more detail in Chapter 9) together with the proposed transferable nil-rate band for spouses mean that even if you already have a will, you should review it.

If you don't have a will, you should make one. So why is having a will so important?

Without a will the assets you leave behind may not go to the people you really want to have them, and the professional costs of winding up your estate are more expensive. If you should die without a will, you die what is known as 'intestate' and there are special rules that govern who will receive your assets. These rules are set out in the table on pages 16 and 17.

If you die intestate, the IHT liability on your estate could be more than it would otherwise be, because the intestacy rules may not make the best use of all the exemptions and reliefs available. A will also enables you to leave instructions, for example about your burial, and gives you the opportunity to nominate who you would like to look after and distribute your estate. You can also say who you would like to be the legal guardians of your children, should the need arise.

The following example shows how dying intestate can mean a larger IHT bill than necessary, because valuable reliefs and exemptions may not be used.

It is even more important for couples who co-habit – rather than being married or in a civil partnership – that a will is made. Otherwise your estate could pass to your parents or other relatives rather than to your long-term partner. All is not lost if you die intestate, as there is an opportunity for the position to be altered within two years of your death through a 'deed of variation' (see page 44). This may be more expensive and upsetting for everyone.

Example: IHT if you die intestate

Mr Hamster dies intestate. He has an estate of £800,000, which includes personal belongings of £15,000. He leaves behind a wife and two young children.

Mrs Hamster will receive the following assets:

	£
Personal chattels	15,000
£125,000 absolutely	125,000
Life interest in 50% of the balance	330,000
Total	£ 470,000

The balance of £330,000 is left on trust for the children. Gifts to a spouse are tax-free so there is no IHT on Mrs Hamster's share of the estate. However, there will be an IHT bill on the children's share as follows:

	£
Taxable estate	330,000
Less: nil-rate band	(300,000)
Taxable estate	£30,000
IHT at 40%	£12,000

If Mr Hamster had made a will leaving more of his estate to his wife, the £12,000 IHT could have been saved.

Intestacy rules

The rules differ depending whether or not you die with 'issue'.
Your 'issue', when looking at the rules below, are your
children and, if they pre-decease you, their children and so on.
If children inherit before the age of 18, their inheritance must
be kept in a 'statutory trust' on their behalf until they reach
that age, or earlier in some circumstances (usually marriage).
Until then, the trust works rather like an accumulation and
maintenance trust, as discussed in Chapter 9.

1) Spouse and issue survive
a) Spouse receives
£125,000 outright
All personal chattels (i.e. belongings but not cash)
Life interest in one half of the residue (i.e. a right to income)

b) Issue receive
One half of residue plus the other half of residue upon death
of spouse

2) Spouse survives without issue
a) Spouse receives
£200,000 outright
All personal chattels
One half of residue outright

b) Remainder shared between
The deceased's parents

If no parent survives:
the deceased's brothers and sisters (but not half-brothers and
half-sisters) and their issue

3) Spouse survives but no issue, parents, brothers or sisters or their issue
Whole estate to surviving spouse

4) No spouse survives
Estate held for the following in the order given. Please note that the person will only benefit if there is nobody in the previous category, or they have all pre-deceased you. For example, your parents will only benefit if you have no issue.

a) Issue of the deceased
b) Parents
c) Brothers and sisters and their issue
d) Half-brothers and half-sisters and their issue
e) Grandparents
f) Uncles and aunts and their issue
g) Half-brothers and half-sisters of the deceased's parents and their issue
h) The Crown, the Duchy of Lancaster or the Duchy of Cornwall

Note that these rules apply to England and Wales – different rules apply in Scotland and Northern Ireland.

Working out your surplus income

Having reviewed the likely IHT and dealt with your will, you might want to consider reducing the tax bill by giving money away during your lifetime. Before you do this, it is necessary to look at your current income position and financial

Checklist of outgoings
These are your likely items of annual expenditure

- Mortgage interest
- Council tax
- Water rates
- Rent
- Gas
- Electricity
- Telephone bill
- House repairs and improvement
- Insurance – home, car, health
- Loan interest
- Maintenance payments
- Holidays
- Subscriptions (gym, golf club, and so on)
- Charitable donations
- Clothes
- Car expenses
- Medical bills
- School fees/childcare
- Food bills
- Spending money, entertainment etc.
- Gifts
- Tax

demands and needs, then decide what you can afford to give away.

As part of this it is necessary to consider your likely items of annual expenditure. Some of these are set out in the table on page 18.

The final step before embarking on any serious IHT planning is to consider your future income requirements. As the example of Mr and Mrs Badger below shows, you have to ensure that there is sufficient wealth to meet future living expenditure, and you must also build in a buffer for the unexpected, for example to meet medical and nursing bills.

Armed with all this information you can now establish

Example: working out surplus income

Let's continue with the example of Mr and Mrs Badger. The example on page 11 shows their capital position. They work out their surplus income for the 2007/08 tax year as follows:

	Mr Badger, £	Mrs Badger, £
Taxable income	195,000	5,000
Tax	(69,500)	(–)
Net spendable income	125,500	5,000
Less: estimated annual expenditure	(82,500)	(1,500)
Surplus income	£43,000	£3,500

This shows that Mr Badger has plenty of surplus income at the moment, but before he gives it all away he needs to think about what his future position will be. How will his income change, for example on retirement? And what will Mrs Badger's position be if he dies before her?

how much you wish to give away to family and friends
during your lifetime.

3

Lifetime giving

As mentioned in Chapter 1, IHT has often been called a voluntary tax. This is because with careful planning, by using the various exemptions, IHT on death can be minimised. The most important and valuable relief is that most gifts made more than seven years before death are exempt from IHT. It is therefore essential to plan early. This is known as the 'seven-year rule' and is discussed further on page 23.

There are also specific exemptions for certain lifetime gifts, for example between spouses. These are covered on page 24.

If you decide to make lifetime gifts, there are a number of potential traps:

- It is not possible to have your cake and eat it. If you give something away, but continue to benefit from it, you may be caught by the provisions for gifts with reservation of benefit – for example if you give your children your house and continue to live there, it will remain within your estate for IHT purposes. These rules are covered on page 30.
- Your gift may be liable for capital gains tax (see page 28).

■ You need to be clear whether the recipient, or your estate, will pay any tax on death (see page 33).

The practical considerations

The best advice in many situations is simply to enjoy your lifestyle, and spend as much as you want. If there is some left for your relatives at the end of it, then all well and good.

The most sophisticated IHT planning is no use to you at all if you have given your capital away and do not have sufficient resources to live on in your old age.

Family relationships must also be considered. Relationships with your children may be good now, but what about in ten years' time? Remember what happened to King Lear.

Think about the consequences of your children getting married or divorced. And think carefully about giving directly to your children at an early age, as they may squander the money or become less independent. This is when trusts may be useful. See Chapter 9 for more information on trusts.

Asset selection

When passing assets to your family, you should examine your capital statement and surplus income (covered in Chapter 2), and decide which assets to gift. If you need to maintain your existing income levels, then consider gifting non-income-producing assets, such as paintings or cars.

While rapidly appreciating assets are good investments, they aggravate the IHT problem by swelling the value of your estate. So it might be advisable to gift these as early as possible.

Generation skipping

When making gifts, you should also consider the IHT position of the recipient. Your children, for example, may be financially secure and you could just be lumbering them with an additional IHT liability. It may be better to make gifts directly to your grandchildren or, if they are young, to a trust set up for their benefit.

The seven-year rule

The seven-year rule applies to lifetime gifts to individuals. It means that the following gifts are tax-free so long as they are made more than seven years before your death:

- Gifts to individuals
- Gifts to bare trust for individuals
- Gifts into a certain type of trust for the disabled

The gifts listed above are known as potentially exempt transfers (PETs) and can give valuable IHT savings, as illustrated in the table on page 24.

Another advantage of making PETs is that although they count as part of your estate, if you die within seven years of making them but survive for at least three years, a special 'taper relief' will apply. This is covered in Chapter 4.

Potential IHT savings on lifetime transfers

Value of estate before gift		Potential reduction in IHT on PETs made more than seven years before death		
£	Gift £100,000	£150,000	£200,000	£250,000
350,000	20,000	20,000	20,000	20,000
400,000	40,000	40,000	40,000	40,000
450,000	40,000	60,000	60,000	60,000
550,000	40,000	60,000	80,000	100,000
1,000,000	40,000	60,000	80,000	100,000

Chargeable lifetime transfers

Note that gifts to trusts other than bare trusts and certain trusts set up for the disabled are not classed as PETs. Instead, they are called chargeable lifetime transfers and there will be an immediate IHT bill if they, plus any chargeable transfers in the previous seven years, exceed the nil-rate band. Any tax payable is charged at a maximum of 20% (the lifetime rate, which is half the rate on death) but more tax may be payable at a later stage – see Chapter 4. Trusts are explained in more detail in Chapter 9.

Tax-free lifetime gifts

There will be no IHT to pay on lifetime gifts which are exempt from IHT and which include the following.

Gifts to a spouse or civil partner

Transfers between a husband and wife – or between civil partners – are exempt from IHT both during their lifetimes and on death. But if your spouse is not 'UK domiciled' (explained in Chapter 12), then only the first £55,000 of the transfer is tax-free. The amount of a lifetime transfer over £55,000 to a non-domiciled spouse counts as a PET.

For this exemption to apply you must be legally married or registered under the Civil Partnership Act and not just living together as co-habitees. As lifetime gifts between individuals are exempt from IHT if they are made more than seven years before the donor's death, the ages of spouses or civil partners should be taken into account when deciding who should make the gift to the intended recipient. If possible, the spouse most likely to survive for seven years should make the gift.

Annual exemption

You are entitled to an annual exemption of £3,000. This means that you can make gifts totalling up to £3,000 tax-free in any one tax year. If you do not use the exemption in one year, it can be carried forward to the next year, but no further. The examples on pages 26 and 67 show how this works.

Small gifts exemption

Gifts of £250 or less to any one individual are tax-free, but this doesn't apply if the total gifts made to that individual in one tax year exceed £250 (so it cannot be combined with the annual exemption). There is no limit to the number of small gifts that you can make to different individuals.

Example: carrying forward the annual exemption

Mrs Ewe makes a gift of £5,000 to her cousin during the 2007/08 tax year. She did not make any gifts during 2006/07. Her position is therefore as follows:

		£
2006/07	No gifts made – exemption to carry forward	3,000
2007/08	Gifts of £5,000 made	5,000
	Annual exemption for 2007/08	(3,000)
	Brought forward from 2006/07	(2,000)

The whole of Mrs Ewe's gift is tax-free, but £1,000 of her 2006/07 exempt amount is unused and its benefit is lost.

Regular gifts out of surplus income

If your income is more than sufficient to meet your annual spending needs (excluding money you save to provide for future needs such as an income in retirement), regular gifts out of your surplus income are tax-free. You should be able to work out how much you can comfortably give away by calculating your net spendable income and setting this against your likely outgoings. In the case of Mr and Mrs Badger on page 19, they have surplus income of £46,500 that they could consider gifting in this way.

It is helpful to have some documentation and calculation in place at the time the gifts are made in order to show that they are made out of surplus income. You do not, however, need the agreement of HMRC before you make the payments; this will normally be dealt with after your death if it is within seven years of the gift, when the personal representatives are agreeing the IHT position.

Gifts on marriage

You can give the following amounts free of IHT to somebody who is getting married:

- Up to £5,000 from each parent
- Up to £2,500 from each grandparent
- Up to £1,000 from any other person

Gifts to charity

Gifts to charity are exempt not only from IHT, but usually also from income tax and capital gains tax. See Chapter 11, 'Charitable giving and philanthropy'.

Other exemptions

- In most cases, gifts for the support and maintenance of children and dependent relatives
- Gifts to a qualifying political party
- A gift for a national purpose (such as a gift to the National Gallery or the British Museum)
- A gift of heritage property or work of art, and so on, even if it remains in private ownership, provided that the public is given reasonable access to it and it is kept in good order
- Maintenance funds for historic buildings

There are certain conditions to be met for some of the above exemptions to apply. It is unlikely that some of these will apply other than in the most extraordinary circumstances. If you have a stately pile then you unquestionably need – but probably already get – specialist help.

Capital gains tax implications

Capital gains tax must also be considered. When you give something away you are treated for tax purposes as if you have sold it, and capital gains tax – a tax on profits made when you dispose of a capital asset – may therefore apply. Broadly speaking, you pay tax on the current market value of the asset, minus its value when you acquired it (its 'base cost'), subject to various reliefs and exemptions.

The tax is currently payable at the same rate as the income tax you pay on your savings income, and the gains are added to your income to calculate the rate due – i.e. at 10 per cent if you are a starting-rate taxpayer, at 22 per cent if you are a basic-rate taxpayer, or 40 per cent if you are a higher-rate taxpayer. However, tax is only payable if your total taxable capital gains in any one tax year come to more than the annual exemption (£9,200 in 2007/08).

The rate of capital gains tax is due to reduce to a flat rate of 18% for disposals which take place on or after 6 April 2008. This change was announced on 9 October 2007 and it means that it may be worth deferring any gifts until after 5 April 2008 if a capital gains tax liability will arise.

Transfers between spouses are tax-free provided the spouses are living together during the relevant tax year.

Care must be taken in the tax year following separation as a capital gains tax charge could arise on disposals of assets between estranged spouses.

Certain assets are free of capital gains tax in any event; for example, cash, motor cars and some yachts.

In some instances, the capital gains tax liability can be

deferred by making a 'holdover' election. The effect of making such an election is that the recipient takes over your base cost for capital gains tax purposes, assuming that no cash passes hands. However, holdover relief can only be claimed on:

■ A gift of 'business assets' by an individual to another individual or trust. Business assets include shares in an unlisted trading company, shares in a quoted company if you own more than 5%, or business assets used for a trade carried on by any such company, or by you as a sole trader.

■ A gift of any assets to most trusts (unless they are trusts where the person who has made or 'settled' the gift has kept an interest, which includes being a beneficiary of the trust and trusts where the beneficiaries are your own not-yet-adult children).

So, in the example below, Mr Squirrel would not be able to claim holdover relief on the gift to his son, but the example on page 30 shows a situation in which holdover relief could be claimed.

Example: capital gains tax on a gift

Mr Squirrel gives a painting worth £50,000 to his son in October 2007. He bought the painting two years earlier at a car boot sale for £50. For capital gains tax purposes, there is a taxable gain of £49,950 arising on the gift. Assuming that Mr Squirrel has already used his annual exemption and is a higher-rate taxpayer, he will have to pay capital gains tax on the gift of £49,950 x 40% = £19,980.

There is no capital gains tax at death, and the beneficiaries of your estate will inherit your assets at the market value at the date of your death. For example, if your house cost £100,000 in 1994 and it is worth £250,000 on your death, your beneficiaries will receive it at a value of £250,000. This will also be their base cost for capital gains tax purposes. Therefore, if they sell the property six months after your death for £260,000, they will only pay capital gains tax on £10,000.

As this shows, you need to weigh up the potential IHT and capital gains tax savings when deciding which assets to give away. It can be a careful balancing act.

Example: holdover relief

Mr Rabbit gives his son his Crazy Carrots Ltd shareholding, which qualifies as a business asset. The current market value of the shares is £150,000 and their original base cost was £50,000, giving rise to a £100,000 capital gain. Holdover relief is claimed, so no capital gains is payable at the time, but when Mr Rabbit Junior eventually parts with the shares, his base cost is also £50,000.

Gifts with reservation of benefit

You may be happy to give your home to your children so long as you may continue to live there for the rest of your life. You may quite like to give your children some cash, but continue to receive the income from it or reserve the right to call the money back if you should need it later in life.

Having your cake and eating it in this way would be ineffective for IHT. A gift is only exempt if it is made outright and with no strings attached. The rules covering what are known as 'gifts with reservation of benefit' are complex and unfortunately it is not possible to go along to HMRC and ask if they apply in any given situation.

If a gift is caught by these rules, then the asset is still deemed to be yours for IHT purposes. It only becomes effective for IHT seven years after you cease to draw any benefit from it. These rules are particularly harsh. As the judge put it in one tax case, 'not only may you not have your cake and eat it, but if you eat more than a few crumbs of what was given, you are deemed for tax purposes to have eaten the lot!'

HMRC has given guidance on the benefits you may receive in respect of property gifted without bringing these rules into play, for example the following would be permitted:

- You give your house to your son and your son lives in it. You may stay there for up to two weeks a year.
- You give a car to your daughter and she gives you occasional lifts in that car (i.e. less than three times a month).

On the other hand, the following are examples of benefits to which HMRC consider that the gift with reservation rules would apply:

- You give your house to your son and then stay there most weekends.
- You give your daughter a car and she gives you a lift to work every day.

There are two situations where you may give something away and still benefit from it without the 'reservation of benefit' rules applying:

- If you pay a full market rent for the use of the land or asset. So, if you give your house to your children but continue to live there, the property will remain in your estate for IHT purposes. However, if you pay your children a full market rent for continuing to live there then the property will no longer form part of the estate. It may be easy to calculate a market rent for a property, but not so easy for assets such as paintings, for example, that you have given away but that continue to hang in your house.
- If you give property to a relative (for example your children), or to your husband's or wife's relative, but then you are forced by age or infirmity, say, to move back in. However, this would only apply if the change in your circumstances was unforeseen when the gift was made, and it represents a reasonable provision for your care and maintenance. This would also apply if, for example, you gave away cash that was subsequently needed for healthcare.

The second exception is unlikely to be of useful practical assistance, although in some circumstances the first exception might be.

If you have entered into an arrangement where you have given away an asset and have continued to have the use of it, but are not caught by the above rules, then it is likely that you will be affected by new law introduced on 6 April 2005.

These rules charge you to income tax in respect of a deemed rental, based on your use of the asset. If you believe that you are caught by these rules, you undoubtedly need professional advice. This new tax is commonly referred to as the pre-owned assets tax.

Who pays the tax?

Finally, when you make a gift, it needs to be made clear who should pay any IHT, if you do not survive for at least seven years. It could be your intention that any tax liability will be paid out of your estate or you may wish any tax charge to be

---

Example: if the estate pays the IHT

Mr Sheep gives £120,000 to his son Lamb. His previous gifts have already used up his nil-rate band. In the event of Mr Sheep's death, he would like the estate to pay any IHT on the gift. He dies within two years of the gift so no taper relief is due. In order to calculate the amount on which tax is payable, the gift is grossed up by two-thirds, as follows:

	£
Gift made by Mr Sheep	120,000
Add ⅔ of £120,000	80,000
Gift subject to IHT (loss to the estate)	200,000
IHT at 40% payable by the estate	£ 80,000

If Mr Sheep had wanted Lamb to pay the tax, the loss to Mr Sheep's estate would be only £120,000. The tax at 40% would be £48,000 and the overall benefit of the gift for Lamb would be £72,000 (£120,000 – £48,000).

met by the person receiving the gift. If you do not make your intentions known, then the recipient will pay the tax. If the recipient does not pay the tax, HMRC will then approach the executors.

Note that the value of the gift for IHT purposes will be the total loss to the estate. If you do not wish the recipient to pay any tax on the gift, and the tax is met from your estate, the taxable amount is the value of the gift itself plus the IHT payable. However, the tax works out at two-thirds of the gift (not 40%), because it is calculated on the loss to the estate (the figures are slightly different if the gift qualifies for taper relief, see page 40). See page 33 for the 'Mr Sheep' example of 'grossing-up', as this calculation is called.

If the recipient is to pay the tax, then the loss to the estate is just the amount of the gift. However, you can take out life insurance that would provide the recipient with enough cash to pay any tax on your death. For more on life insurance see Chapter 5.

4

On death

IF YOU HAVE A WILL, you have probably nominated executors to deal with your estate on your death. Otherwise, your estate will pass in accordance with the rules on intestacy (see Chapter 2) and your heirs will be appointed to act as administrators. Your executors or administrators are called 'personal representatives' and are responsible for:

- valuing your estate and working out the tax on it (see below)
- claiming any appropriate reliefs or exemptions (see page 39)
- paying any IHT due. Payment is due within six months of your death. This can give rise to difficulties for some personal representatives, for example where the main asset of the estate is the family home. But see page 42 for various ways of funding the tax.

Valuing your estate

The personal representatives dealing with your estate will need to make the fullest possible enquiries into your affairs in order to ascertain its value. By going through the papers and making enquiries on what may be the slimmest of leads they will piece together a picture of the estate. If you are acting as a personal representative then the Probate Service website (www.hmcourts-services.gov.uk) can explain how to apply for probate, and will supply forms and advise on their completion. Further information can be found on the HMRC website (www.hmrc.gov.uk).

The personal representatives will submit form IHT200 to HMRC Capital Taxes to give details of the assets and liabilities at the date of death (your estate). The personal representatives can deal with the papers themselves, or they can instruct a solicitor – or in some cases an accountant – to do so on their behalf. If your estate is able to make a claim to transfer a dead spouse's unused nil-rate band (see page 12), then the personal representatives will also need to complete form IHT216 and send it with the IHT200 form.

Schedules attached to form IHT200 will provide details of assets that you gave away in the seven years prior to death. These are included at their market value at the date of the gift, but if their value has fallen since then, the market value at the date of death can be used instead. (If the value of the asset has increased no adjustment is required.) Gifts of assets from which you still benefited ('gifts with reservation of benefit') must be included. As explained in Chapter 3, these remain part of your estate for IHT purposes.

You may also have had an 'interest in possession' in trust funds (see Chapter 9). The trust funds in which you have an interest that commenced before 22 March 2006 (or in certain cases before 6 April 2008) count as part of your estate for calculating your IHT liability. The trustees will return details of the interest in the trust fund using form IHT100b.

All of the values that are returned on these forms are added together to give your chargeable estate on death. Deductions are made for any reliefs, the nil-rate band and transferred nil-rate band (using the figure that applies in the tax year of death – £300,000 for deaths in the 2007/08 tax year). The rest of your estate, after deductions, is charged to IHT at the rate of 40%.

Excepted estates

After 1 September 2006, if you die leaving an estate of £285,000 or less, you need to complete another less detailed form instead of form IHT200. The limit of £285,000 applies for deaths occurring after 5 April 2006 and is subject to change from time to time.

There are restrictions to the use of the excepted estates arrangements. For example, these arrangements are not available if more than £150,000 of your estate is represented by trust property or if property of more than £100,000 is situated outside the UK. Additionally, they will not apply if you have made gifts of more than £150,000 in the seven years before your death.

Who pays the tax?

The recipient of a lifetime gift (PET) is liable to pay any IHT due on the gift on your death, unless you have made arrangements for the tax to be met out of the estate (see page 33).

Example: how much tax?

Mr Monkey died in May 2007, leaving an estate of £750,000. He had a life interest in a trust fund (created in 1990) of £250,000. He had also made PETs of £300,000 within the previous seven years. The total tax due is £400,000.

	Chargeable amount, £	Tax, £
PETs made within seven years of death	300,000	
Less: nil-rate band available	(300,000)	
	Nil	
Estate on death	750,000	
Trust fund in which Mr Monkey had a life interest	250,000	
	£1,000,000	
	@ 40% =	400,000

Tax on death

The IHT due is apportioned as follows between the estate and the trustees.

Tax on estate

$£400,000 \times \dfrac{£750,000}{£1,000,000} = £300,000$

Payable by personal representatives

Tax on trust fund

$£400,000 \times \dfrac{£250,000}{£1,000,000} = £100,000$

Payable by trustees

The same applies if you have transferred money to a trust that was a PET before 22 March 2006 – the trustees are liable. Your personal representatives are liable to pay any other tax. If more than one person is liable to pay the tax due, the overall IHT charge is split between them in line with the proportion of the estate to which they are entitled. This is demonstrated in the example opposite.

Chargeable lifetime transfers

It was mentioned in Chapter 3 that IHT may be payable during your lifetime on gifts into most trusts, at the lifetime rate of 20%, if you have already used up the nil-rate band. Any such gifts that were made within seven years of death become part of the net chargeable estate on which tax at 40% will be paid. An allowance is made for the tax paid previously at the lifetime rates.

Warning: exempt and non-exempt legacies

Where the balance of your estate, after specific legacies have been made, is left to some beneficiaries who enjoy exempt status (your spouse and charities, for example) and others who are not exempt, it is advisable to say in your will how the IHT is to be allocated. In the absence of specific directions making it clear that the tax burden is not to fall on the exempt beneficiaries, they will be left paying part of the tax.

Exemptions and reliefs

Tax-free gifts on death
The following gifts which are exempt from IHT if made in

your lifetime – and which are covered elsewhere in this book
– are also tax free on death:

- Gifts to a spouse or civil partner – see page 25
- Charitable bequests – see page 27
- Business property relief – see page 63
- Agricultural property relief – see page 96
- Woodlands – see page 96
- Assets of national importance – see page 97

Taper relief
If you made gifts within the seven years prior to your death

**Example: taper relief on gifts within seven years of
death**

Mrs Bear gives assets worth £325,000 to her son, having
made no previous gifts. They are worth £375,000 when she
dies four and a half years later.

	Chargeable amount, £	*Tax, £*
Chargeable gift	325,000	
Less nil-rate band	300,000	
	25,000	@ 40% = 10,000
Less: taper relief of 40%		(4,000)
IHT payable		£6,000

Note that the gift is pooled with all the other assets of your
estate and does not attract an additional nil-rate band. As the
gift has used up all of Mrs Bear's nil-rate band, the whole of
her estate at death will be subject to IHT at 40%.

---

they will become chargeable to IHT when you die. If the total of the gifts is within the nil-rate band then there will be no tax to pay on those gifts, but if a liability does arise the tax payable on gifts made between three and seven years of death will be reduced as follows:

Period between gift and death	Rate of reduction in tax liability
3–4 years	20%
4–5 years	40%
5–6 years	60%
6–7 years	80%

Quick succession relief

Relief is given for those situations where someone dies within five years of inheriting assets on which IHT has been paid. To avoid a second burden of IHT on the same assets, a proportion of the IHT paid on the first death will be deducted from the tax charge due on the second death.

Example: succession relief

Mr Gerbil has a chargeable estate of £500,000. On his death, his estate includes a painting worth £150,000, which was valued at £100,000 two and a half years earlier when it was left to him by his father. On his father's death IHT of £40,000 was paid on the painting.

	£
IHT on Mr Gerbil's estate of £500,000	80,000
Less: Relief for tax paid on painting by father's estate	(14,400)
Total IHT payable by Mr Gerbil's estate	£65,600

The proportion of the tax relieved is calculated using a formula to which the following percentages are applied:

Period between deaths	Relief
Less than 1 year	100%
1–2 years	80%
2–3 years	60%
3–4 years	40%
4–5 years	20%

Assets that fall in value

Relief may be claimed for some assets sold within a short period of your death, at a value that is lower than the probate value. This applies to certain qualifying investments (such as quoted shares) sold within a year of your death, or to land or property sold within three years of your death. In these cases the sale proceeds may be taken as the basis for working out the IHT, instead of the probate value. The claim must relate to all of the qualifying investments sold, not just those sold at a loss.

Funding the IHT

When the application is made for the grant of probate, the personal representatives have to make an initial payment of IHT. This initial payment does not include the liability on any freehold property or on any assets for which they are claiming to pay by instalments.

The personal representatives may have to organise a loan for the payment of the tax. But this may not be necessary if the estate includes money in accounts with banks and building societies which belong to the Direct Payment Scheme. This enables money to be paid from the relevant account(s) direct to HMRC without probate having to be granted. An IHT bill can also be settled using British Government Stocks and/or National Savings & Investment products – including Premium Bonds – held in the estate.

Paying by instalments

Your personal representatives can elect to pay the IHT over a period of ten years by ten equal annual instalments. Interest is payable on the outstanding amount. This option only applies to certain assets as follows:

- Land (including the family home);
- Shares of a company in which you had control;
- Unquoted shares if payment of tax would give rise to hardship;
- A business, interest in a business, or unquoted shares worth at least £20,000 if their nominal value represents more than 10% of the total nominal value;
- Unquoted shares held at your death, provided that at least 20% of the total tax payable relates to these shares or to other assets for which tax can be paid by instalments.

If IHT is payable on a gift you made in the seven years before your death, the asset you gave away must still be held by the recipient for the instalment method to be claimed. If the relevant property has been sold, the outstanding tax (and interest) is payable immediately.

Acceptance in lieu

HMRC can accept important heritage objects in lieu of IHT. It may accept works of art, manuscripts and historic documents. Further information can be found at www.resource. gov.uk/action.ail

Deeds of variation

Within two years of the date of your death, it is possible for your beneficiaries and your personal representatives to execute a deed of variation to change the provisions in your will or the allocation of assets if you die intestate. For the purposes of calculating IHT, the redistribution will be treated as having been made by you.

This procedure enables a person who does not wish to receive a legacy from your estate to give the funds to someone else, and the usual seven-year survival period does not apply.

Professional advice should be taken before entering into a deed of variation and consideration should be given to the income tax and capital gains tax implications of such an arrangement.

However, do not rely on deeds of variation as a substitute for writing a will. Governments have on various occasions considered their removal and you should not rely on them being around in the future.

A variation of a will which includes gifts to minor or unborn children can only be made by an application to the courts, which can be expensive.

5

The role of insurance

EVEN IF YOU ARE ABLE TO MAKE use of all the available exemptions and reliefs from IHT discussed in the previous chapters, there is still a risk that there will be an IHT bill on your death. You may be able to give away some assets to reduce the potential tax bill, but when you die your estate may still include the family home and savings set aside to meet expenses in old age. To reduce the risk that your heirs will have to pay a substantial tax bill, one option is to take out a life insurance policy to fund the estimated IHT bill on death.

The two types of life insurance most commonly used in conjunction with IHT planning are 'term' and 'whole-of-life' policies.

Term insurance

Term insurance is the simplest form of life cover; it is called term insurance because it covers a specified period or term. If you die during the policy term (and assuming all premiums due have been paid), the policy will pay out the sum specified in the policy. If you survive beyond the policy term, you don't get anything. The term is decided at the outset and can be anything from a few days to several decades. Premiums are also set at the outset and do not normally change over the life of the policy. However, premiums may increase if the policy gives you the option to extend the term or the option to convert it to a whole-of-life plan.

You can take out a term insurance policy on either a single or joint-life basis. Term insurance is generally the cheapest form of life cover and, for IHT-planning purposes, it may be suitable when the requirement for meeting any tax liability is linked to a specific term – such as the seven-year IHT liability on any potentially exempt transfers (PETs) – see Chapter 3.

Whole-of-life insurance

As the name suggests, a whole-of-life policy can provide cover for the whole of your life – provided the premiums are paid – and not just for a fixed term.

Like term insurance policies, you can apply to take out a whole-of-life policy on either a single- or joint-life basis. It is generally cheaper to buy a joint-life policy – rather than two single-life policies. It is these joint-life policies that are most commonly used for IHT planning.

Whole-of-life policies tend to be more complex than term policies but they can also be more flexible. Many whole-of-life policies are linked to an investment fund. The premiums you pay buy units in the investment fund some of which are sold to pay for a specified level of life cover. If the underlying investment fund performs in line with expectations, premiums are unlikely to change substantially over the life of the policy. But if the investment fund underperforms, premiums may have to go up to ensure that there continues to be enough money in the policy to pay for the specified amount of life cover. The alternative is to reduce the amount of cover.

There are many different types of whole-of-life policy. They can have different review dates, and the premium costs can vary. You should always investigate what is the right policy for your own circumstances.

Buying a policy

With both types of policy, what you pay in premiums depends on a number of factors including:

- The amount of life cover required
- Whether the policy is single or joint life
- Your age, gender and general state of health.

If you plan to include buying insurance as part of your overall IHT planning, the most important thing you need to know is what the potential tax bill is estimated to be. Without this vital information (see Chapter 2 for guidance in calculating an IHT bill), you won't know how much life cover you need to buy. It is important to review your life cover periodically to make sure it is adequate to cover your IHT bill.

You will also need to consider whether the policy should cover just your life or whether – as is common for couples – you should cover both your lives using a joint-life policy. With a joint-life policy, you also need to decide when you want it to pay out. If there will be an IHT bill only on the second death, a policy written on a 'joint-life last-survivor' basis would be the most appropriate.

Finally, as with any kind of insurance where your state of health is a factor in deciding premiums, you may also need to undergo a comprehensive medical examination before taking out a policy.

Writing policies in trust

Any life policy – whether it is a term or whole-of-life policy – is usually written 'in trust'. This means that when you die and the policy pays out, the proceeds are paid to the trustees, who will exercise their discretion as to who should receive the money – and in what proportion. It is usual to provide a letter of wishes indicating who you would like to benefit. This is not a legally binding document, but the trustees will generally follow your wishes. Writing a policy in trust is usually simply a case of using the insurance company's standard documentation. However, in some cases – and in the light of changes to the taxation of trusts – it may be more appropriate to get advice from a trust specialist.

There are two advantages of writing a policy in trust. First, policy proceeds are paid out upon production of the death certificate so there is no need to wait for probate to be granted which avoids any delay in the money being paid. Second, proceeds do not usually form part of your estate and so do not attract IHT. You should therefore give serious consideration to asking trustees to pay the proceeds of a life policy to your children and grandchildren. If they are paid to your spouse, although there is no immediate IHT bill, the

> ### Example: insuring against an IHT bill
> Mr and Mrs Feline estimate that, after taking account of all available reliefs and allowances, the IHT bill on their estate would be £500,000. They don't want to make gifts while they are still alive because they feel that they may need the assets to provide them with cash when they are older. Although there will be no IHT bill when the first of them dies, there could be an estimated bill of £500,000 on the second death. To cover this amount, they could take out a whole-of-life policy on a joint-life last-survivor basis with a sum assured of £500,000 – the amount of their estimated IHT bill. Mr and Mrs Feline also make sure, by writing the policy in trust, that the policy proceeds don't add to their estate.

proceeds will fall into your spouse's estate on his or her death and any potential tax saving will be lost.

If you make your children and/or grandchildren the beneficiaries of a life policy, the annual premiums you pay for the policy may be treated as chargeable lifetime transfers (see page 24) for IHT purposes. However, there is unlikely to be a tax bill as the premiums will either fall within the £3,000 annual gifts' exemption or count as tax free because they are treated as a regular gift out of surplus income (see page 26). You may, therefore, need expert advice if premiums are very expensive.

Other ways to use insurance for IHT planning

As well as providing a lump sum to cover any potential IHT bill, insurance can also form the basis of other flexible and innovative approaches both to general estate planning and to gifting money on your death.

The use of the insurance-based investment bonds described below as part of a strategy for making gifts can be very effective in saving IHT. Not only do these policies tend to be straightforward from an administrative point of view, but they can be a tax-efficient 'wrapper' within which to hold a portfolio of investments. A particular attraction when investing in unit-linked funds through an insurance bond is that any switch between funds held in the bond will not give rise to an immediate tax charge (although special rules can apply to offshore investment bonds). This flexibility is of particular benefit for trustees who may be investing over very long periods and who may therefore want to adjust their investment strategy periodically.

Using investment bonds

Investment bonds are single-premium life assurance contracts through which you can invest into the life company's own funds, or into a portfolio of collective investments – such as unit trusts and open-ended investment companies (OEICs). The investment value will be paid out on the death of the life assured, sometimes with additional life cover. The advantage of investing through an investment bond – rather than directly in unit trusts or OEICs – is that because an investment bond is based on life insurance, different tax rules apply. For example, if you were to gift units in a unit trust to someone other than your spouse, you might trigger a capital gains tax liability. However, you can usually assign an investment bond to someone without triggering a chargeable gain, provided that you do not receive money or money's worth in return. If you assign an investment bond to someone under a bare trust (see Chapter 9), the transfer will count as a PET (see Chapter 3) and so there will be no IHT to pay if you survive for seven years after the transfer.

Alternatively, a bond can be assigned into a flexible (discretionary) trust, although this may trigger an immediate IHT bill. This enables the trustees to choose who will benefit from the trust at a later date.

The proceeds from a single premium investment bond will be subject to income tax on any gains when a chargeable event arises. As death of the last life assured is a chargeable event, this could give rise to an income tax charge. The exact amount of tax due, if any, will depend on a number of factors and can differ between onshore and offshore investment bonds.

Discounted gift trusts

Assigning an investment bond can mean relinquishing all control over your money. So if you want to retain some access to capital, a suitable alternative might be to set up a discounted gift trust which is also available from insurance companies. The way it works is that an investment bond is put into trust for named beneficiaries. But your gift to the trust carries the right for you to make regular withdrawals from the bond. This right creates a 'discount' which is calculated by an actuary and based on your age, gender and health at the time of setting the trust up. For IHT purposes, the

Example: how a discounted gift trust can help reduce an IHT bill

Mr and Mrs Terrier – aged 71 and 65 respectively – are both in good health and have every prospect of living for at least seven more years. They have £700,000 that they would like to go to their three children but from which they would like to continue to draw an income – in this case up to £35,000 a year.

Mr and Mrs Terrier will each contribute £350,000 to the purchase of the investment bond. But because of their different ages, the discounts calculated by the insurance company's actuary (and agreed by HMRC) also differ. As Mr Terrier is older and likely to die before his wife, his likely total withdrawals will be lower than Mrs Terrier's and so his discount is also lower than hers .

The Terriers' gifts into the trust will be as follows:

Total sum to be invested:	£700,000
Each invests half:	£350,000
Value of Mr Terrier's gifts after the discount:	£170,000
Value of Mrs Terrier's gifts after the discount:	£110,000
Total value of gifts for IHT purposes	£280,000

The total discount is £420,000 (that is, the original investments totalling £700,000 less the value of the gifts for IHT purposes of £170,000 and £110,000). If both Mr and Mrs Terrier were to die unexpectedly shortly after investing, the IHT saving could be as much as £168,000 if their nil-rate band was used up on other assets in their estate.

They have chosen to put the bond into a discretionary trust to give them flexibility later on as they may wish to give some of their estate to their grandchildren. This type of trust could produce an immediate IHT bill but as both of the gifts after the discount fall within the nil-rate band of £300,000 for each person, there is no tax to pay. Without the discounts, both

> would have incurred a tax charge on the £50,000 over the nil-rate band – a saving for both Mr and Mrs Terrier of £20,000. Their annual 'income' (the withdrawal of 5%) from the bond will be tax deferred for the first 20 years.

discount has the effect of reducing the value of your gift. These schemes can immediately reduce your potential IHT liability while allowing you to take cash from the bond for the remainder of your life – assuming there is still money in the bond to withdraw. However, because discounted gift trusts are underwritten at the outset, the discount will not normally be worthwhile unless you are in good health. Unlike outright gifts, the beneficiaries of these schemes will not have access to any capital until your death.

Loan trusts

You might want to consider a loan trust if you want to retain capital, but would like future growth from that capital to fall outside your estate for IHT purposes on death. Loan trusts are typically offered by insurance companies and comprise an interest-free loan to a trust which is used to purchase an investment bond. Unlike a discounted gift trust, you can request full or partial repayment of the loan at any point. Repayment of the loan would be in the form of withdrawals from the bond (assuming it hasn't fallen in value to be worth less than the amount of the outstanding loan). As you have access to the original capital at all times, the money lent to the trust still forms part of your estate for IHT purposes.

Example: how loan trusts work

Mrs Beagle is 45 years old and has two children. She is a high earner and has spare cash of £100,000. However, although she has no immediate use for the money, she and her husband still want access to this capital and also want to be able to draw income from it.

She decides to invest in a loan trust by lending the £100,000 to a discretionary trust. The loan is used by the trustees to buy an investment bond from an insurance company. Each year, the trustees can pay Mrs Beagle 5% of the bond free of tax. Withdrawing at this rate would mean that the original loan is repaid after 20 years.

Mrs Beagle withdraws 5% every year but the bond grows on average by 7% each year. After twenty years the loan has been fully repaid but despite the yearly withdrawals, the investment, after charges, has accumulated a value in the trust of just over £100,000. When Mrs Beagle dies, this sum does not form part of Mrs Beagle's estate and so the trustees can distribute it free of IHT.

However, on death only the original loan – minus any repayments from the trust – is added to your estate. Any growth in the value of the bond does not count towards the calculation of IHT. (See the example above.) Once again, these can be complex areas, and you should always discuss such investments with your professional adviser.

6

The family home

WITH THE MASSIVE INCREASE in property prices over recent years, the family home is causing a real headache for many in terms of IHT. If, as shown in the example on page 56, the remainder of your estate is not sufficient to cover the IHT liability, this can present your dependants with a real practical problem, because the tax is due just six months after your death. There is an option to pay by instalments (see Chapter 4), but in some cases, failure to plan carefully for the potential tax bill will mean that the family home has to be sold to pay the tax. This may not be what you and your family want.

According to Land Registry records, in July 2007 the average price of a detached house in Greater London was £604,743, while the average price of a terraced house was £313,580. Average prices of detached houses in both the South East and South West also exceeded the nil-rate band, which is currently £300,000.

The value of your family home, after deducting any mortgage on the property, falls into your estate for IHT purposes. There are no general exemptions available. However, the sale of your main residence is not usually subject to capital gains

Example: practical problems with property

Mr Horse, a widowed man, dies on 11 April 2007, leaving the following assets to his two children:

	£
House	450,000
Cash	55,000
	505,000
IHT on: £300,000 (the nil-rate band)	Nil
£205,000 @ 40%	82,000
IHT due on 1 November 2007	82,000

As you can see, there is pressure on the children to sell the house before 1 November in order to pay the IHT. Otherwise they could consider paying the tax by instalments.

tax. This is because there is a special 'main residence' exemption in respect of the family home. If you own more than one property, specialist advice should be obtained to ensure that the maximum capital gains tax relief can be claimed.

Simple planning

IHT planning around the family home has always been considered 'last-resort planning'. Apart from the financial security a home offers, the emotional ties can be considerable too.

For IHT purposes, you cannot simply give your house to your children and continue to live there rent-free. The complex rules concerning 'gifts with reservation of benefit' (covered on page 30) mean that the value of the house will remain within your estate. One way to get round this is to pay your children a full market rent but this means taking on the risks of being a tenant and being at the mercy of your children!

Appropriate planning will depend upon your circumstances and a strategy that suits you may not suit your neighbour.

Borrowing against your home

As discussed in Chapter 5, you could choose to take out life insurance to cover the potential IHT liability. Alternatively, with interest rates currently reasonably low, you may decide to take out a fixed-rate mortgage on your property. The mortgage will reduce the value of the house for IHT purposes, but the cash raised would swell the value of your estate. To get round this you would need to remove the cash raised by the mortgage from your estate. You could simply give your children the cash and provided you survive seven years there will be no IHT to pay on the gift. You need to weigh up the cost of the mortgage interest against the likely tax saving.

Alternatively, you could use the cash to invest in assets that qualify for business property relief: for example, shares in your family trading company or shares in an unquoted trading company. Business property relief is explained in further detail in Chapters 7 and 10. Provided you hold those shares for two years and all the other conditions are met, the relief will wipe out any liability to IHT on those assets. The commercial considerations of this route clearly need to be taken into account – you would be in a mess if you bought shares in companies that collapsed.

Selling your property to your children

If your children have sufficient funds you could sell your house to them for its market value and then in due course remove the cash from your estate, as outlined above. Your children could then allow you to live in the property rent-free, but you would, of course, be at the mercy of your children. Assuming the property was sold for more than £125,000 (in the 2007/08 tax year), your children would also have to pay stamp duty land tax. The capital gains tax implications must also be considered, as your children cannot claim the main residence exemption if they do not live in the property. Additionally, this has become more complex due to new income tax laws introduced on 6 April 2005 (see page 32), and therefore further advice should be sought.

Changing the way you own your home

Married couples usually own their home as joint tenants. This means that on your death, the house automatically passes to your spouse. As you are married, there is no IHT to pay on the first death. Although administratively this is the simplest route, in the past it would have cost your family up to £120,000 in tax, because you are not making use of your nil-rate band. When your spouse dies his or her estate will be increased by the value of the house. However, not making use of the nil-rate band on the death of the first spouse may no longer be a problem now that a spouse can effectively inherit an unused nil-rate band (see page 12).

You could think about converting your joint tenancy so that you own the property as tenants in common. This enables each of you to leave your share of the property to someone other than your husband or wife, thereby making use of your nil-rate band. However, there is always the problem with being tenants in common that a joint owner can force a sale of the property.

If you are unsure whether you own your property as joint tenants or as tenants in common, your solicitor will be able to tell you. Note that different rules apply in Scotland (but not in Northern Ireland).

Unmarried couples

Only married couples and those in civil partnerships can inherit from each other free of IHT. If you are an unmarried couple living together, there is no IHT exemption available, even if you own property as joint tenants – although you will still automatically own the whole home on the death of the other joint tenant.

If you have a joint tenancy but want to leave your share of the property to someone other than the other joint owner, you will need to sever the joint tenancy and become tenants in common. This will enable you to leave your share in the property to whomever you wish (provided you make a will – see Chapter 2). For example, your will could provide for your share in the property to be transferred to your niece, but with your partner having the right to live there until his or her death. There are no particular IHT savings in this route, although it may be preferable from a family viewpoint. There are also risks with this strategy, as your partner might not feel comfortable with the idea of living in a property of which one half is owned by your niece.

More complex planning

Before 6 April 2005, it was possible to exploit other, more complex, arrangements for IHT planning around the family home which in very basic terms involved giving money to children to buy your home from you but allowed you to continue living there. However, since that date, the introduction of a special income-tax charge means that it is likely that – although still effective for saving IHT – these arrangements now carry an income-tax cost which may both be expensive and outweigh the IHT benefit. There was an option to elect for the family home to be included in your estate, but the deadline for doing this was 31 January 2007. If you think you may have entered into one of these complex arrangements with your home, you should seek professional advice.

A second property

If you own more than one property, your tax planning not only needs to take account of the potential IHT liability but also of a possible capital gains tax bill. This is because when you sell or give away property which isn't your main home you do not qualify for main residence relief and so any lifetime gift of property may mean paying capital gains tax.

Having said that, when buying the property a suitable structure for ownership should be considered.

For example, you may wish to put money into a trust for your grandchildren, which the trustees use to acquire the property. If the amount you give to the trust is within your available nil-rate band (currently £300,000) and you survive for seven years, your nil-rate band will revive and you can do the same thing every seven years.

You should seek specialist advice in this area, particularly if you intend to stay at the second property from time to time, in case you are caught by the 'gifts with reservation of benefit' and pre-owned assets tax rules, as explained on pages 30–33.

The overseas property

More and more of us are buying properties overseas. This can have many traps for the unwary. For example, France has rules stipulating who should receive certain property on your death, irrespective of what your will says. This means that your French 'chateau' may not necessarily pass in accordance with your wishes on your death. Many overseas jurisdictions have annual wealth taxes and gift taxes with which we are unfamiliar in the UK. Some countries will charge you tax on the sale of the property, even if you are not resident there. It is essential when you are purchasing a property overseas to appoint a local lawyer with good English skills. You may also require a local will that deals specifically with the property in that country.

Acquiring a property overseas through a company may get

around problems with local taxes. Traditionally, properties in Spain and Portugal were acquired through an 'offshore tax haven' company for local reasons. However, this can in some limited circumstances give rise to income tax problems in the UK if not structured correctly. Owning the property via a trust or a trust arrangement may solve your problems, but again caution is the word, as many civil law countries just do not understand what a trust is.

Generally speaking, in the case of property there will be some form of tax on death to pay in the local jurisdiction, unless you are lucky enough to own a property in a country where there are no taxes at death, such as many of the Caribbean Islands. If you are worried about your executors having to pay tax in the other jurisdiction, do not despair. HMRC will usually allow such taxes to be offset against your UK IHT bill. You should seek specialist advice as this is a very complex area.

7

The family business

IF YOU OWN SHARES in a family company your IHT affairs need to be considered and planned very carefully, as the value of your shares may form a large part of your estate.

The financial position of future generations may be dependent not only on the profitability and success of the company but also on careful IHT planning. Failure to plan could mean that some or all of the shares will have to be sold to pay the tax and the family would lose control of the business.

Business property relief

IHT on the shares in your family company can cause problems if the company is very profitable and the market value of the shares is very high. Business property relief is, therefore, a very important and valuable relief. There are two rates of relief: 100% and 50%.

Relief at 100% is available for the following assets:

- A business or interest in a business, i.e. sole trader or partnership;

■ Any shares in an unquoted trading company; this includes
shares listed on the Alternative Investment Market (AIM).

Relief at 50% is available for the following assets:

■ Shares in a quoted company that you control;
■ Any land or building, plant or machinery that is used
wholly or mainly for the purposes of a business carried on
by a company which you control or by a partnership of
which you are a partner;
■ Any land or building, plant or machinery used wholly or
mainly for the purpose of a business you carry on, that is
held by a trust of which you are a life tenant.

Business property relief is not available where the business
consists wholly or mainly of:

■ Dealing in securities, stock or shares;
■ Dealing in land or buildings;
■ The making or holding of investments.

These are called 'excepted assets'. An asset that is not used
wholly or mainly for the purpose of the business concerned
can also become an excepted asset, and relief is restricted in
line with business use (see example on page 65).

In order to qualify for relief on business property you
must have owned the asset in question for at least two years.
There are special rules for replacement assets.

It is therefore important to consider carefully whether all
the conditions for relief are met, whether the company is a

Example: business property relief

Mr Lion makes a gift of an 80% unquoted shareholding in the family trading company to a discretionary trust, in January 2003. This qualifies for 100% business property relief.

The company has been successful and the market value of the holding is £1.5m. At the date of the transfer the company owns assets worth £1.5m, of which £0.25m consists of the chairman's yacht. The yacht is an excepted asset for IHT purposes and so the relief is restricted in line with the proportion of excepted assets. Only $^{1.25}/_{1.5}$ of the full relief is available.

Mr Lion's gift, for tax purposes, is:

	£
Value of shares	1,500,000
Less: business property relief $^{1.25}/_{1.5}$ x 1,500,000 x 100%	1,250,000
Gift for tax purposes	250,000

A gift to a trust is a chargeable lifetime transfer (see page 24) and so it is taxable immediately if it (plus previous taxable gifts) exceeds the nil-rate band. Clearly if Mr Lion's nil-rate band has already been used, the potential IHT charge is significant.

qualifying business for these purposes, and whether the value of any business property arises from 'excepted assets'.

Lifetime gifts

Shares in the family company are ideal assets to give away early. If the company is successful the shares are also likely to appreciate in value and are valuable assets in the hands of the recipients and this needs to be balanced with the fact that the base cost of the shares would be uplifted to market value on death (see page 30).

You need to consider the capital gains tax implications of giving away shares, but holdover relief for capital gains tax (explained on page 29) may be available. You also need to think about whether your income is likely to be affected by a fall in your shareholding, if the company distributes profits to shareholders by way of dividends. You could instead draw profits by way of a salary to ensure that your level of income is maintained, but this may have adverse National Insurance implications.

Another practical problem may arise if you wish to ensure that you do not jeopardise your control over the company's major policy decisions. This position can be overcome by gifting your shares into a trust. If you are a trustee you can still control the voting rights of the shares.

A gift to a trust may be taxable immediately, if full business property relief is not available. Types of trust are explained further in Chapter 9. In this way, the shares can be passed on for the benefit of your family without you losing voting control. It could also ensure that the shares do not need to be sold to pay IHT on death. Holdover relief for capital gains tax purposes (see page 29) may be available on the gift into the trust.

Another way of protecting against IHT on shares is to gift them to a charitable trust formed by the family. The value of the shares is taken outside the family as the shares are held for charitable purposes, but, again, voting control is maintained.

Example: the business property relief trap

Mr Tiger gives an 80% unquoted shareholding in the family company valued at £500,000 to his son, Thomas, in November 2003. As Mr Tiger didn't use his £3,000 annual exemption in either that year or the previous one (see page 25), £6,000 of the gift is immediately tax free. The rest of the gift is taxable if Mr Tiger dies within 7 years, but it is potentially eligible for 100% business property relief. Thomas sells the shares in June 2006 and keeps the cash.

When Mr Tiger dies in October 2008 the gift becomes taxable and business property relief is denied as Thomas has sold the shares. However, it qualifies for taper relief at 40% because Mr Tiger survived for 4 years (see page 40). Mr Tiger's estate is comprised of a house valued at £200,000 (which is tax free because he left it to his wife) and other investments valued at £30,000, left to his son.

The IHT position on death is shown below.

Chargeable amount, £		*Tax, £*
PET now chargeable	494,000	
IHT on	300,000 (the nil-rate band)	Nil
	194,000 @ 40% =	77,600
Less taper relief @ 40%		(31,040)
Tax on gift of shares		46,540
Estate at death	30,000 @ 40% =	12,000
Total IHT due on death		£58,540

The family would be left with a tax liability of £58,540 on Mr Tiger's death and assets may need to be sold to pay this. If Thomas had retained the shares or acquired replacement property that qualified for business property relief no IHT would have been payable.

A trap for lifetime transfers

As the example on page 67 shows, even if the conditions for granting business property relief are satisfied at the date of the original gift, failure to meet these conditions at death results in the denial of the relief.

A gift of business property should therefore be considered closely. For example, if you have given away shares that qualify for relief at the time of the gift and then die within seven years, the value of the gift is still included in the calculation of the IHT liability (although it may qualify for taper relief). The value of the gift will only be reduced by business property relief if the recipient still owns the shares (or has replaced them with other qualifying assets) and they still qualify for relief.

Therefore, if at the time of your death (if this occurs within seven years of making the gift) the recipient has sold the shares, there will be no business property relief available when calculating the IHT due.

Valuation

In the case of shares in an unquoted family company, the problem is that there is no open market value for the shares. It is, therefore, necessary to undertake a share valuation.

There are many techniques for valuing shares but the important factor is that the value should reflect a hypothetical open market price that a willing buyer would pay a willing seller.

In calculating the taxable amount of a share transfer it is

Example: valuing unquoted shares

Mr Hedgehog owns all the issued share capital in a company valued at £1m. He wishes to gift a 30% interest to a trust, leaving him with 70%. The agreed discounts which may normally be negotiated with HMRC might be as follows:

Shareholding, %	Discount, %
100	0
70	10
30	50

The value of the gift is as follows:

	£
Value of Mr Hedgehog's holding before gift: £1m @ 100%	1,000,000
Value of Mr Hedgehog's holding after gift: £1m @ 70% less 10% discount	630,000
Transfer for IHT purposes	£370,000
However, the value of the assets held by the trust is: £1m @ 30% less 50% discount	£150,000

necessary to look at the value of your shareholding before and after the transfer. A discount will also need to be applied to shareholdings of less than 100% of the issued share capital of the company. This is because a 5% shareholding is worth less than 5% of the value of the company, as its voting rights have very little influence over the affairs of the company. Such valuations can sometimes provide surprising results, as the example above shows.

Buy and sell agreements

A final word of caution is due in respect of buy and sell agreements. It is common for partners or shareholder directors to agree that in the event of your death before retirement your personal representatives are obliged to sell and the survivors are obliged to purchase your shares. If you enter into such an agreement, then business property relief may be denied.

8

Pensions

PENSIONS REMAIN ONE of the most popular ways of saving for retirement. Largely because of tax relief on pension contributions, they offer a tax-efficient way of building up capital which is then used to provide an income in retirement. Pensions can also provide some welcome IHT benefits.

Pension simplification

On 6 April 2006, the government introduced new rules to simplify the various different – and highly complex – sets of rules that had grown up to govern what you could pay into a pension and what you could take out at retirement. For example, before the new rules came into force, you could pay only a maximum of 15% of salary into an employer's pension scheme but anything from a maximum of 17.5% to 40% into a personal pension plan.

Under the new rules, whether you are paying into an employer's scheme, a personal or stakeholder pension, or a self-invested personal pension (SIPP), you can receive tax relief for pension contributions up to 100% of your annual income, subject to an annual limit of £225,000 in 2007/08

and £235,000 in 2008/09. All pension contributions are
made after deducting basic-rate tax of 22%, so a £100 contribution costs only £78. From 6 April 2008, these will
change to 20% and £80 respectively. Higher-rate tax payers
get up to 40% tax relief, which brings the cost after tax relief
of a £100 contribution down to £60. Even non-tax payers
qualify for basic-rate tax relief and anyone, whether earning
or not, can pay up to £2,808 a year – topped up to £3,600
by the government – into a personal or stakeholder pension.

The new rules also raised the minimum age at which you
can take your pension from 50 to 55 from 2010. However,
retiring earlier than age 55 will still be possible on the
grounds of serious ill health.

The lifetime allowance

The new rules also put a ceiling on the amount of pension
savings that qualify for tax relief in your lifetime. In the
2007/08 tax year, this lifetime allowance – which will rise
each year by a fixed amount until 2010, when HMRC will
review the position – was set at £1.6 million. If, when you
come to draw your pension, the total value of all your
pension funds exceeds the lifetime allowance in force at the
time, the amount above the limit will be taxed at an effective
rate of 55%. The total value of your pension funds includes
the value of benefits from a final-salary scheme. These are
valued at a rate of £20 for every £1 of promised income.

Investors with very large existing pension funds can make
a claim to be protected from the charge of 55% on funds in
excess of the lifetime allowance. However, whether such pro-

tection will be granted depends both on the value of *all* pension assets at 6 April 2006 and on whether any further contributions have been made. Applications for protection must be made by 5 April 2009.

Your pension at retirement

At the point that you decide to take an income from your pension fund, you will also be given the option of taking a tax-free lump sum. The maximum amount of tax-free cash you can take is usually 25% of the pension fund. The remainder of the pension fund must be used to provide an income which is taxable.

Options for providing a pension income

There are a number of options available when you come to take a pension at retirement. Because the decision you make at this point will affect your income for the rest of your life, it is vital that you get independent advice from an adviser with specialist training.

The basic choice is between a secured and an unsecured arrangement for providing your pension.

Secured pensions include the purchase of an annuity where you part with your pension fund in return for a regular income which is guaranteed to be paid until your death.

With an unsecured pension arrangement, you draw an income (within limits set down by HMRC) directly from your pension fund, which remains invested.

Which of these options you choose depends upon a

number of factors, but your choice will be influenced by:

- The size of your pension fund
- Your attitude to investment risk
- How keen you are on flexibility – particularly concerning what you can pass on when you die

While unsecured pension arrangements, without doubt, carry a higher level of risk they do offer a more flexible way in which to draw retirement benefits. But because the pension fund remains invested, the success or otherwise of an investment strategy that follows the unsecured route will very much depend upon any investment growth achieved.

IHT implications on pension benefits paid on death

Given the amount of capital that is tied up in pension funds, their value upon death can be substantial. For this reason, you need to understand what steps you can take to ensure that your pension fund falls outside your estate for the purposes of IHT. It may be possible, for example, to write your pension policy in trust so that death benefits do not fall directly into your estate on death.

Alternatively, for older pension arrangements or company schemes, you may need to complete an expression of wish form indicating to the pension trustees who you would like to benefit from your pension fund (and in what proportion) on your death.

Given the different types of pension arrangement and the ways in which they are set up, you should always seek

detailed guidance on the best way to plan in order to min-
imise any IHT liability.

In general, the current death benefit rules are more flexible than those that were in place before the simplified rules
for pensions came into force on 6 April 2006. How the rules
treat the tax position of death benefits depends on whether
you have already started taking retirement benefits or have
yet to do so – called 'uncrystallised rights'. But typically,
death benefits from a pension, whether already being paid or
not, must be paid either as a survivor's pension or as a lump
sum.

IHT if you have yet to draw pension benefits

If you have not already started taking an income from your
pension, you need to compare the amount of your fund to
the lifetime allowance to see what tax charge there is. If the
amount of death benefit payable is greater than the lifetime
allowance at that time, your beneficiary will face a 55% tax
charge on the excess. This position may be different if you
have elected for protection from the lifetime allowance
charge (known as either primary or enhanced protection).
Importantly, death benefits paid from a registered pension
scheme before age 75 should normally be free of any liability
to IHT, although in some cases there must be an appropriate
underlying trust in place to avoid death benefits being paid
directly into your estate.

IHT if you have already started to draw pension benefits

If you choose an annuity, death benefits will typically be
limited to either a spouse's or dependant's pension or the

continued payment of the pension you were receiving for a specified number of years. This 'guarantee period' normally lasts for either 5 or 10 years.

Alternatively, if you choose to draw an income from an unsecured pension arrangement and die before age 75, it is possible for death benefits to be paid as a lump sum. This is based on the value of the fund at the time of your death and is subject to a 35% tax charge – known as a special death benefits tax charge. There is no tax charge if your dependants choose to take an ongoing income from the fund rather than a lump sum. Clearly, this option is suitable only for dependants who are prepared to take some risk with the income they get from your pension after your death – so they should be sure to take detailed financial advice before making a decision.

The position changes again once you reach the age of 75. At this point you must choose between buying an annuity or drawing benefits using an alternatively secured pension. If you choose the alternatively secured pension route, then, following your death, any dependant will have choices depending on their age – but not normally including the option to receive a lump sum. The choices are either to buy an annuity or, if under 75, to take an unsecured pension – or, if over 75, to choose an alternatively secured pension. If you have no dependants, the fund can be paid free of IHT to a registered charity. The fund may also be able to be transferred to other scheme members, but the total tax charges will almost certainly be severe.

This is a highly simplified description of a complex area on which you are strongly urged to take professional advice.

There are certain exceptions to the treatment of death benefits which may lead to a charge to IHT if HMRC decides that a person in ill health delayed taking pension withdrawals, reduced his or her income payments or made other benefit choices purely to increase benefits paid to dependants on death.

9

Trusts and their investment issues

TRUSTS ARE USED for a variety of reasons. In the past, trusts were often used as a way of avoiding tax. But as the tax benefits of trusts have largely disappeared, trusts are now used more for family reasons. For example if you wish to pass capital down to another generation, using a trust will allow you to maintain control over when and how much your child or grandchild has to spend.

The Finance Act 2006 (FA 2006) introduced radical changes to the IHT treatment of trusts. The rule changes affect both new trusts set up after 22 March 2006 and trusts already in existence before that date.

The new rules mean that (with some exceptions; see page 24) any gift you make to a trust that you set up in your lifetime is immediately chargeable to IHT if it exceeds your nil-rate band (currently £300,000).

Why bother with a trust?

Although the IHT treatment of trusts has changed, there will still be good family reasons for setting up a trust. A trust offers a suitable vehicle for passing capital to the younger generation while keeping control over it.

It is important to remember that when you set up some types of trust you are actually giving your assets away and they will no longer belong to you. Your solicitor or other appropriate adviser will be able to draw up a trust deed for your requirements and you should consider who you would like to be trustees. You may wish to be a trustee yourself and it's always advisable to appoint an independent person such as a family accountant or solicitor to be a trustee alongside family members.

The Society of Trusts and Estate Practitioners has some useful information on its website www.STEP.org and the HMRC website www.hmrc.gov.uk also has some useful guidance.

Types of trust

Which type of trust you choose will depend largely on when you want the beneficiaries of the trust to receive the assets held in the trust and how flexible you want the trust to be.

Bare trust

This is the most straightforward but least flexible sort of trust. Under a bare trust only the beneficiary is entitled to the capital and all of the income. A bare trust is usually used if the beneficiary is under 18 and the trust funds are being held on his or her behalf by adult trustees until the beneficiary is old enough to take control of the money. For example, the opening of a bank account in your child's name is a bare trust. Once the beneficiary is over 18 years old, he or she can insist at any time that he or she takes control of the assets.

Because of the favourable way in which bare trusts are taxed (see 'How trusts are taxed' on page 82), they are a useful tool for IHT planning. If, for example, you wish to give cash to your grandchildren but do not want them to have access to it until they are 18 you can put the money into a bare trust. Provided you survive seven years from making the gift to the trust, there will be no IHT on the gift. However, note that while your children (but not grandchildren) are under 18, you will continue to be liable to pay income tax on any income arising on gifts made by you to them.

Interest-in-possession trust

Under an interest-in-possession trust, a beneficiary has a limited interest in the trust funds, such as an interest in a share of the trust income for life or for a period of years – to age 35, say. After the interest comes to an end, a further interest in the income may pass to someone else or another beneficiary may become entitled to the assets.

A beneficiary who is entitled to a share of the trust income is said to have an 'interest in possession' in the trust fund. But unlike a bare trust, for interest-in-possession trusts set up since 21 March 2006, the assets held in the trust do not form part of the beneficiary's estate. Before 21 March 2006, if you set up an interest-in-possession trust in your lifetime, the assets in the trust were considered to belong to the beneficiary for IHT purposes.

An interest-in-possession trust is useful if you would like

your child to be entitled to a regular income but not entitled to the actual capital until later on in life. For example, if you have remarried but have children from a previous marriage, you may wish to protect your spouse during his or her lifetime but ensure that your wealth passes to your own, rather than your spouse's, children on death.

Discretionary trust

The discretionary trust is the most flexible of all the types of trust. The settlor can leave his or her options open by gifting wealth into a trust and naming a list of beneficiaries whom he or she might like to benefit in the future. All of the beneficiaries do not have to have been born at the time the trust is set up and you can name a 'class' of beneficiary such as your children or grandchildren. How money in the trust is shared out between the beneficiaries is left to the discretion of the trustees.

Accumulation and maintenance trust

An accumulation and maintenance trust is a special sort of discretionary trust and is particularly suited to making gifts to children who are under 25.

Initially the trust will be discretionary in nature, because it is set up for a pool of beneficiaries (usually grandchildren) and income can be paid out for their maintenance at the discretion of the trustees. Any income not paid out is accumulated within the trust.

How trusts are taxed

The transfer of the cash and assets into a bare trust count as
a gift to an individual and so as a PET (see page 23) for the
purposes of IHT. So if you survive for seven years after
setting up a bare trust, there is no IHT to pay. Transfers of
assets – such as shares – into a trust count as a disposal for the
purpose of capital gains tax so there may be capital gains to
pay. But once any assets have been placed in the trust, they
then form part of the beneficiary's estate for IHT.

Since 22 March 2006, the transfer of assets into an interest-in-possession trust, accumulation and maintenance trust
or discretionary trust counts as a chargeable gift. So anything put into a trust over the nil-rate band of £300,000 is
subject to a 20% IHT charge. The 20% charge applies both
to assets put into the trust when set up and to further gifts
to the trust made at a later date. There is also an additional
charge of up to 6% on everything over the nil-rate band
every 10 years and a further maximum 6% charge on everything over the nil-rate band when the trust finally pays out
the money held in it.

However, trusts which have 'protected status' (see page
83) do not have to pay the ten-yearly charge.

Tax on trusts set up before 22 March 2006
Interest-in-possession and accumulation and maintenance
trusts created before 22 March 2006 will gradually be
brought into the new IHT-charging regime although transitional rules for such trusts have provided opportunities to
vary their terms in order to preserve their more favourable

IHT status. For example, if you alter an accumulation and maintenance trust so that the trust funds are paid to the beneficiaries at age 18, the trust retains the same favourable tax treatment as a bare trust. The transitional period comes to an end on 5 April 2008.

The scope of this book does not cover these transitional provisions in detail and if you are a trustee, a beneficiary or settlor of a trust created before 22 March 2006 you should seek professional advice and a review of the trust so that any amendments can be made before the deadline of 6 April 2008 expires.

Trusts with protected status

Trusts for a disabled person – whether set up on death or by lifetime gift – are exempt from the new IHT tax charge. This is also true of certain trusts created under a will – or by intestacy – since 22 March 2006 which have special 'protected status'. This means that they will not be subject to the same IHT regime as trusts set up in someone's lifetime.

The three new types of trusts which are given special protected status are:

- Immediate-post-death-interest trusts
- Trusts for bereaved minors
- Age 18–25 trusts

Immediate-post-death-interest trusts

This new sort of trust is essentially an interest-in-possession trust. The difference is in the tax treatment. The assets in the

trust remain in the beneficiary's estate and are not subject to
the 10-year and exit charges.

Trusts for bereaved minors

A trust for a bereaved child who is under 18 can be created
only by a parent and only in the parent's will. The terms of
the trust must say that the beneficiary becomes absolutely
entitled to a share of the trust property at age 18. Again no
10-year or exit charges will apply.

Age 18 to 25 trusts

An 18–25 trust arises where the beneficiary does not take an
absolute interest at 18 but the trust continues until the age of
25. The trust will not be subject to 10-year anniversary
charges and will not be subject to exit charges while the beneficiary is under 18 years of age. Between the ages of 18 and
25 a charge will arise of up to a maximum of 4.2% of the
assets passing absolutely to the beneficiary.

Investment issues for trustees

Trusts can be used for IHT planning in situations where
someone wants to remove assets from his or her estate by
giving them away but at the same time retain some control over
the money. This can be particularly useful where assets are
shares in a family company or where the proposed beneficiaries
are too young or inexperienced to manage the assets themselves. Another way in which the use of a trust can be useful is
where someone is undecided about who will eventually benefit
from the trust but keen to remove assets from his or her estate.

The role of the trustees

Given that trusts are typically set up to exercise a level of control over gifts to future generations, the role of trustees in identifying an appropriate investment policy and carrying it out efficiently is an important one.

Trustees are governed by The Trustee Act 2000 which came into force on 1 February 2001 in England and Wales.

Duty of care
The Trustee Act introduced a new statutory duty of care, aimed at bringing certainty and consistency to the standard of competence and behaviour expected of trustees. This duty of care was brought in as an addition to the other fundamental duties of trustees (detailed in the table below).

Duties of a trustee
1. To take reasonable care in exercising their duties
2. To read and understand the trust deed
3. To act fairly between beneficiaries
4. To comply with the terms of the trust
5. To provide information and accounts to the beneficiaries on request
6. To decide and act unanimously with other trustees
7. To act without reward – unless a professional adviser
8. Not to make secret profit from the trust
9. Not to purchase trust property
10. To invest fund assets in accordance with the trust deed
11. To disclose any potential conflicts of interest

Source: Commentators on Trustee Act 2000

General power of investment

Trustees now have the power to invest in the same range of investments as if they were the absolute owners of the assets. This power gives trustees the widest possible investment choice while their duty of care ensures that they act prudently in safeguarding the capital of a trust. In practical terms, this means that trustees must have due regard for the suitability and appropriateness of investments and must take professional investment advice where appropriate. In order to meet these investment obligations many trustees find that it is helpful to draw up a statement of investment policy. A written policy statement both helps an investment manager to draw up the best strategy to fulfil the trust's objectives and helps the trustees to review investment performance over time.

This means that trustees should:

- Establish the objectives of the trust and review these on a regular basis
- Establish and review the investment policy in conjunction with an investment professional (if appropriate)
- Agree in writing an investment policy setting relevant performance benchmarks and review dates (see table on page 87).

Choosing an investment adviser

Trustees are required to seek professional investment advice where appropriate, but it isn't compulsory. If, as trustees, you feel confident making investment decisions yourself, you may decide to invest directly or to use a professional adviser on an

What should a statement of investment policy cover?

1. The trust's overall objectives
2. The investment objectives in terms of income and capital appreciation, including anticipated capital additions/withdrawals
3. The approach/tolerance to risk
4. The broad investment strategy
5. Investment time horizon
6. The day-to-day management of the investments
7. Investment restrictions and constraints
8. Investment benchmarks/performance measurement criteria
9. Review periods
10. Other tax and legal constraints

This list is not necessarily exhaustive

execution-only basis where he or she carries out your instructions but you carry the responsibility if things go wrong.

Making investment decisions yourself may be appropriate where you don't have much money to invest and the cost of employing a professional would eat heavily into the trust fund. Alternatively, the trust's investment objectives may be very risk averse, thereby limiting you to choosing investments that don't require as much professional advice – such as cash savings accounts.

However, if you would prefer to delegate your investment decisions to an investment professional, you first need to decide whether you want to use a discretionary management or an advisory management service. The differences between the two are outlined below.

Discretionary management

Under this type of arrangement you sign an investment management agreement to give an investment manager the authority to buy and sell investments without having to obtain your approval before each transaction. The investment manager can make these investment decisions on your behalf once you have agreed your objectives, the time frame to achieve them and your risk profile in a written mandate, which forms part of the investment management agreement.

Having an investment management agreement in place means that because the investment manager doesn't have to contact you before making each investment decision, the manager is able to react quickly to investment opportunities and changes in the market. Transactions for all the investment manager's clients can also be carried out in bulk, which potentially reduces costs.

Advisory management

Your investment manager will be contracted to keep investments under review and to make investment recommendations whenever they consider it appropriate based on the risk profile and objectives that you specify. Choosing advisory management simply means that no transactions will take place without your express approval – either verbally or in writing. Advisory management is therefore a slower process than a discretionary arrangement, but it offers a greater level of control while retaining the ability to take advantage of someone else's research.

Investment manager checklist

1. What is the size and ownership structure of the investment manager, where is it based and who regulates it?

2. Does the investment manager have experience of looking after clients with circumstances such as yours and what is its policy towards the qualifications of its portfolio managers?

3. Does the investment manager conduct all its own research or is research bought in from third parties?

4. Can the manager offer you a broadly diversified portfolio across different asset classes (such as equities, fixed interest securities, property and alternative investment assets)?

5. Does the manager invest directly in shares, use funds such as unit trusts which themselves invest in shares, or employ a combination of both?

6. What resources does the manager have at its disposal?

7. What risk controls are in place?

8. Who looks after your portfolio of investments when your portfolio manager is on holiday or otherwise absent from the office?

9. What custody and administration services can the manager provide? Do these meet your requirements?

10. Can the manager provide your tax advisers with a consolidated tax statement?

11. How often will you receive a written performance report and meet the portfolio manager?

This list is not necessarily exhaustive

What to look for in an investment manager

Once you have decided to use the services of an investment manager, it is important that you are able to select a manager who has the necessary skills to assist you in achieving your investment objectives.

While there are a number of detailed points that you should consider, the checklist on page 89 may prove a useful guide in cutting through the jargon and finding the right adviser for you.

While this may seem a complex and involved process, by taking some time to meet different investment managers and establishing their approach towards managing assets, you are more likely to find the right mix of investment acumen and personal attention.

Reviewing your investments

There are a number of ways to measure the performance of investment managers, the most common of which is to use an independent performance benchmark. A comparison against this can show how well your manager has done relative to other managers or assets that make up the selected benchmark.

Among the issues to consider when reviewing an investment manager's performance are:

- Has the portfolio achieved its stated objectives?
- How has it performed against the performance benchmark?

> **Example: keeping investments under review**
> Mr Doberman has invested in a portfolio of UK equities for long-term capital growth. Over the past 12 months his portfolio has risen in value by 6%. Over the same period, the FTSE All Share index has risen by 8%. Therefore Mr Doberman's portfolio has under-performed the benchmark by 2%.

- Has the manager taken excessive risk to achieve your aims?
- Have any restrictions placed on the investments been acknowledged and adhered to?

By reviewing the portfolio on a regular basis – most private investors and trustees choose to review their portfolios at least annually – you will be able to keep on top of any performance trends and identify if you need to take any action such as revising investment objectives or restrictions or alternatively appointing a different investment manager.

10

Tax-efficient investments

HAVING DETERMINED THE VALUE of your estate and the potential IHT bill, it is worth reviewing the assets that make up your estate. You may not wish to give away any assets during your lifetime, but you could be interested in changing their mix in your estate to help reduce the tax due when you die.

There are a number of investments which can offer substantial IHT planning benefits in their own right. In particular, investments that benefit from business property relief – such as certain companies listed on the Alternative Investment Market, woodland and certain property ventures – offer prospective investors a combination of a potential return on their capital while reducing their estates after the investment has been held for two years. Some of these arrangements can be very complex and nearly all of them require a substantial minimum investment – typically £50,000. They are therefore aimed at relatively wealthy investors and should never be entered into without detailed and expert professional advice.

By acquiring assets that give rise to IHT relief and disposing of assets that do not, the value of your estate may not change but the tax charge may fall. The assets that attract relief are set out in this chapter. Of course, you must keep in mind the capital gains tax consequences outlined on page 28, as well as considering the commercial implications, in order to ensure that the assets acquired will be suitable investments in other respects. As the old adage goes, 'Don't let the tax tail wag the investment dog.'

Some tax-efficient investments are described below, but if you are considering acquiring or already own them, you will unquestionably need specialist advice.

Business property

As explained in Chapter 7, investments in some types of business property qualify for relief of up to 100%. This includes shares listed on the Alternative Investment Market. The benefit from investing money in business property can be seen from the example of Mr Elephant on page 94.

If you own 'unquoted shares' in a company, they are treated in the same way as your own business or interest in a business. Because shares listed on the Alternative Investment Market are seen by HMRC as 'unquoted', the same relief applies. Relief on such assets is 100% of the IHT liability after you have held them for a minimum of two years. This means that the value of your capital falls outside your estate after that period, provided you maintain your investment in assets that also qualify for the relief.

Of course, these reliefs are given in return for the risk you take investing in small businesses. Although some companies on the Alternative Investment Market are now quite large, most of them are newer, riskier businesses than those quoted on the main London Stock Exchange.

One way of managing this risk is to invest in a portfolio of shares on the Alternative Investment Market that is overseen by an investment manager with experience in this market. The manager should take care of the qualification rules for you and ensure that any trades he makes do not lose your relief should you die unexpectedly.

While shares quoted on the Alternative Investment Market may provide a shelter for IHT, you must take specialist advice as to the suitability of this type of share as an investment.

Example: investing in business property

Mr Elephant owns assets of £900,000, made up of his house and a bank deposit. The IHT due on his estate would be £240,000. If he invested some of his assets in shares in the Alternative Investment Market instead, which qualify for 100% business property relief, then his ultimate IHT liability may be reduced as follows:

Assets	Original estate	Reinvested estate
AIM shares	–	£250,000
House & contents	£500,000	£500,000
Bank deposit	£400,000	£150,000
Total estate	£900,000	£900,000
Less assets qualifying for 100% relief	Nil	(£250,000)
Less nil-rate band	(£300,000)	(£300,000)
Taxable estate	£600,000	£350,000
IHT @ 40%	£240,000	£140,000
Potential tax saving		£100,000

Enterprise Investment Scheme

The Enterprise Investment Scheme (EIS) allows very small, often start-up, companies to offer new shareholders a number of tax reliefs. Among these potential benefits, EIS company shares qualify for IHT business property relief.

EIS qualifying companies, by their very nature, are almost always high-risk investments. However, there are investments using EIS qualifying companies that have been specially designed to reduce IHT while lowering much of the investment risk.

For such deals, the returns will generally be low, but the providers of the investments assume that your objective is to obtain IHT relief rather than high returns on speculative ventures. If you are considering using business property relief, you could well investigate this area with your adviser.

Trading companies

Since business property relief applies to your own business, it is possible to set up a trading company, or companies, to pass on your wealth free of IHT. As with the EIS concept of lower risk/low return discussed above, your trading company would invest, along with other similar companies, in specially selected business projects. Such projects could be property construction, operating pubs or buying tracts of managed woodland (see page 96 for other uses of this type of investment). The returns may not be exciting, but again the overriding objective is obtaining IHT relief while preserving capital.

Farms

If you own a farm this may attract agricultural property relief at either 100% or 50%. The definition of a farm is fairly wide. It includes farm buildings and farmhouses, together with the land occupied with them, if they are of a character appropriate to the property. However, this area is complex and you should take specialist advice.

The breeding and rearing of horses on a stud farm and the grazing of horses in connection with those activities also qualify for agricultural property relief. This includes any buildings used in connection with those activities.

In order to get relief, you must have occupied the property for agricultural purposes for at least two years. Alternatively, if the property is used by somebody else for agricultural purposes, you must have owned it for seven years.

You will be entitled to agricultural property relief at 100% if you have the right to vacant possession (or the right to obtain vacant possession within twelve months). Otherwise, 50% relief is due.

Woodlands

The acquisition of a woodlands estate is a long-term investment (normally a minimum of ten years), but it can provide valuable IHT savings. Woodlands can be acquired at various stages of development – indeed, certain trees can take 50 years to reach their full size. The work involved would normally be undertaken by professional forestry managers.

For IHT purposes, 100% of the value of the standing timber may attract relief, making it effectively tax-free provided you have owned it for two years. A commercially run woodlands investment is worth considering if you wish to pass wealth to your family in a tax-efficient manner.

A woodland or forestry plantation that is managed in order to produce timber should also qualify for business property relief. Wealthy investors can acquire an estate as a long-term investment which will be free of IHT on their death. The production of timber also carries certain income tax and capital gains tax benefits.

It is now also possible to participate in woodlands investments with lower levels of capital, usually by contributing to a trust which manages the woodland professionally. This structure may allow heirs to sell your participation to a new investor.

Lloyd's underwriters

If you are a Lloyd's underwriter you will qualify for business property relief at 100% on all assets contained in the Lloyd's business, and also for property subject to Lloyd's deposit guarantees.

Heritage land and buildings

If you own certain heritage assets then these are exempt from IHT, provided you allow reasonable public access to them and undertake to maintain and preserve the property. The assets must also stay within the UK.

The types of asset that this exemption might apply to are:

Summary of some tax-efficient investments

Type of Scheme	IHT relief	Other tax benefits	Main risks
Alternative Investment Market portfolio	IHT BPR gives 100% relief after 2 years holding the investment. Investor retains control of the asset throughout	None	AIM market falls – loss of capital offsets IHT saving. Liquidity of small company stocks – meaning that it may be difficult to find a buyer
Enterprise Investment Schemes structure		Initial income tax relief and capital gains tax benefits	EIS carry small-company risk of business failure. Liquidity – meaning that it may be difficult to find a buyer
Certain trading companies		None	Small-company risk of business failure. Liquidity – meaning that it may be difficult to find a buyer
Woodlands		No income tax or capital gains tax on timber production	Timber prices fall – hence value of investment and ability to re-sell. Liquidity. Uninsurable risks to the timber produced
Family home – equity release and home-reversion plans	In general, no IHT relief, although there are some planning opportunities	None	Could leave estate with an outstanding debt on the home or no value in the home for heirs

This is a summary of some key issues and is not exhaustive. You should always seek detailed advice before selecting any option.

- Works of art and other objects of national scientific, historic or artistic interest
- Land of outstanding scenic, historic or scientific interest
- Buildings (and objects associated with such buildings) of outstanding historic and architectural interest

Home reversion and equity release plans

Equity release plans were designed to allow you to obtain cash from the value of your home and thereby enhance or maintain your current standard of living. There are many variations on offer, but the two main types are 'lifetime mortgages' and 'home reversions'.

If you own your home outright, you can obtain a lump sum or income by taking out a lifetime mortgage on which you make no repayments. The sum borrowed rolls up with interest to produce a debt against your estate when you die. If you dispose of the money raised so that it is not in your estate, the debt should reduce the IHT liability on your death, but of course it also reduces what you leave your heirs. You will only be able to borrow a proportion of the equity mortgaged, because you retain ownership and hence the right to live in the house. The final debt could exceed the value of your house, though safeguards against this for your heirs are usually built in.

With a home reversion plan, you sell either all or part of your property to an insurance company or bank in return for a lifetime right to continue living in it. This takes the part of the property sold out of your estate for IHT. Again, the value of the lump sum (or income stream) you receive will be much less than the market value of the property, because you have the right to continue living in the house for life. You also lose flexibility to raise more money at a later date or to repay the money raised.

While this type of planning can be effective, there are substantial risks (as well as emotional considerations) to bear in mind, and you should get relevant professional advice before proceeding.

11

Charitable giving and philanthropy

ANY GIFT TO A CHARITY that is registered with the Charities'
Commission which you make, either during your lifetime or
in your will, is free of IHT. This means that making gifts to
charity can be a useful way of reducing the taxable value of
your estate for IHT purposes.

As well as being free of IHT, gifts to charity offer other tax
benefits depending on the scheme.

- Gift Aid – both one-off and regular payments to charity of
  any amount qualify for tax relief under the gift aid scheme
- Payroll giving schemes operated by employers provide tax
  relief on donations made via the payroll
- Donations of assets or investments which can be made
  either to existing charities or to a charity set up by the
  individual or company making the gift

A donor who wishes to make substantial gifts over a
period of time or carry out specific charitable activities may
prefer to set up their own charity.

What to look for in a charity

At the end of September 2007 over 90% of all charitable donations was committed to 8% of all registered charities (source: Charities' Commission). It may be, however, that individuals or families who want to make charitable gifts or donations wish to support more specific causes.

In this respect, it is helpful to define a strategy for your giving – deciding on where to focus the giving and establish criteria by which to select charities. This is an area to which few people give detailed thought.

Given the sheer range of options available, it is important to research the background of different charities prior to making a gift and it is essential to check that a charity is registered with the Charities' Commission. While a charity may be efficient it may not necessarily deliver the benefits that you as a donor would wish to achieve. This can happen when a charity does not have a clear strategy or vision.

Donors often benefit from thinking carefully about why they have chosen to give. Some may wish to reflect their personal values, or involve their families. Others may want an active involvement in any charitable causes that they support.

For example, donors may wish to support advocacy charities which work to shape policy and influence change on a national scale or they could support charities which work on an individual level, providing far more quantifiable and immediate results into the community. Ironically, giving money away effectively can be a lot more difficult than making it. One of the world's greatest investors and philanthropists, Warren Buffett, concluded that the most effective solution was to hand over his money to someone else to do the giving – and he chose the Bill and Melinda Gates Foundation.

An example of how to create a giving strategy would be to answer the following questions:

- What do I want my donations to achieve and how should they reflect my values?
- How do I like my family to be involved in decisions and the management of my giving?
- Are there specific causes or geographical locations that I wish to support?
- Which of the various types of charities or charitable activities do I wish to support?

12

The overseas element

THE UK HAS OFTEN BEEN DESCRIBED as a tax haven for those coming to live here from abroad. It has a peculiar tax system that gives certain tax benefits if you are 'domiciled' outside the UK.

Most people are familiar with the rules relating to residence (i.e. where you live on a day-to-day basis), but broadly speaking domicile means where you have your long-term connections and where you consider is home (see page 105).

IHT is geared towards domicile rather than residence:

- If you are domiciled in the UK, you are subject to IHT on your worldwide assets
- If you are domiciled overseas, you are chargeable to IHT on your UK-sited assets only

Often the opportunity to take advantage of not being domiciled in the UK is overlooked. But with careful planning, your IHT bill can be substantially reduced. Remember, though, that if you are UK domiciled the spouse exemption is reduced to £55,000 if your spouse is non-domiciled (see page 25).

Possible reform

HMRC is reviewing the tax rules in relation to non-domiciled individuals. So now is the time for you to review your position and plan accordingly, before any changes are introduced. It is currently proposed that any change in the rules will come into effect from 6 April 2008.

What is domicile?

The term domicile is a matter of general law. Its rules are different from those of residence and should not be confused with nationality or citizenship.

When you are born, you acquire a domicile of origin, which is usually your father's domicile at the time of your birth. (This is not the case if you are illegitimate or born after your father's death, in which case you take your mother's domicile.) Your domicile then follows that of your father until the age of sixteen. A domicile of origin sticks to you like glue and it's quite hard to shake off. You will acquire a domicile of choice in the UK if you move here and intend to stay permanently or indefinitely. There are special rules for women who married before 1 January 1974.

In some cases, it may be possible to ask HMRC for a ruling on whether you count as non-domiciled. However, in most instances you would complete your Self Assessment Tax Return certifying that you consider yourself to be non-domiciled. HMRC is of course entitled to challenge your domicile position.

Deemed domicile

Even if you are not UK domiciled, for IHT purposes you are deemed to be domiciled in the UK if you have been resident in the UK for seventeen of the last twenty years of assessment, or if you were domiciled in the UK in the three years before a chargeable transfer. These rules present certain traps for the unwary. For example, you are deemed resident for a tax year, even if you are only present in the UK for part of that year.

Example: deemed domicile

Mr Zebra moved to the UK on 4 April 1992, and has been resident here for tax purposes ever since.

He is counted as resident under these rules in the 1991/92 tax year, even though he was only here for two days. He will therefore be treated as deemed domiciled with effect from 6 April 2007.

If he had arrived two days later, he would not have been treated as deemed domiciled until 6 April 2008.

On becoming deemed domiciled, your worldwide assets become subject to UK IHT. It is therefore important that your affairs are planned properly before you become deemed domiciled.

One possible planning idea is to 'break' your deemed domicile status. This would involve you leaving the UK for four tax years. Return visits to the UK (within strict limits) are allowed during that period.

> ### Example: breaking your deemed domicile
> Mr Raccoon became deemed domiciled on 6 April 2004. He decides to leave the UK on 31 March 2005 and returns on 10 April 2009. He has broken his deemed domicile position and the twenty-year clock starts again on 6 April 2009.

Basic planning

If you are not domiciled in the UK, you may still have assets here, even after you have left the country. If you should die, those assets remain subject to IHT. By rearranging your wealth, substantial savings can be made.

> ### Example: rearranging assets to save tax
> Miss Armadillo is non-UK domiciled. Shortly after returning to her home in Sweden, she passed away, leaving the following UK assets.
>
> | | £ |
> | --- | --- |
> | UK property | 230,000 |
> | UK bank deposit | 180,000 |
> | UK quoted shares | 100,000 |
> | Total UK estate | £510,000 |
> | IHT on: £300,000 (the nil-rate band) | Nil |
> | £210,000 @ 40% | 84,000 |
>
> This IHT liability could easily have been avoided by transferring the UK bank deposit to an overseas account, selling some of the UK quoted shares and reinvesting in overseas securities (subject to commercial considerations, of course!).

The use of trusts

The use of trusts is of particular importance if you are non-UK domiciled. This is because any overseas assets you transfer into an offshore trust are excluded from charge to IHT, even if you subsequently become deemed domiciled in the UK. However, this rule is currently under consideration by HMRC.

Example: using an offshore trust

Mr Wallaby is domiciled in Australia. He will become deemed domiciled for IHT purposes on 6 April 2008. He has overseas assets of £4m. Before 6 April 2008, Mr Wallaby settles an offshore trust and transfers those assets to it. The assets should then remain outside the UK IHT net, even when Mr Wallaby becomes deemed domiciled.

Obviously the income tax and capital gains tax implications also need to be considered.

Useful information

IHT rates 2007/08

On death	*Rate of tax*
£0 – £300,000	Nil
Over £300,000	40%

During lifetime (i.e. on transfers to a discretionary trust)	*Rate of tax*
£0 – £300,000	Nil
Over £300,000	20%

The nil-rate band will be increased to £312,000 in 2008/09 and to £325,000 in 2009/10. At present, the rate of tax is unchanged.

Taper relief for lifetime gifts

Period between transfer and death	*Rate of reduction in tax liability*
0–3 years	0%
3–4 years	20%
4–5 years	40%
5–6 years	60%
6–7 years	80%

HMRC leaflets

IHT2	'Inheritance Tax on lifetime gifts'
IHT3	'Inheritance Tax. An introduction'
IHT12	'Inheritance Tax. When is an Excepted Estate Grant appropriate?'
IHT12(S)	'Inheritance Tax. When is an Excepted Estate Grant appropriate?' (The rules in Scotland)
IHT14	'Inheritance Tax. The personal representatives' responsibilities'
IR45	'What to do about tax when someone dies'

Addresses and websites

BDO Stoy Hayward LLP
55 Baker Street
London W1U 7EU
Telephone: 0870 567 5678
Fax: 020 7487 3686
www.bdo.co.uk

The Chartered Institute of Taxation
12 Upper Belgrave Street
London SW1X 8BB
Telephone: 020 7235 9381
Fax: 020 7235 2562
www.tax.org.uk

The Society of Trust and Estate Tax Practitioners
26 Grosvenor Gardens
London SW1W 0GT
Telephone: 020 7738 4890
Fax: 020 7738 4886
www.step.org

HMRC (Probate and IHT helpline)
Telephone: 0845 302 0900
www.hmrc.gov.uk

Other BDO titles are listed on the following pages

Finance Directors
A BDO Stoy Hayward Guide for Growing Businesses
by Rupert Merson

What is the role of the finance director in a smaller or medium-sized business with ambitions to grow? And what is the experience of working as a finance director in an entrepreneurial environment actually like?

Rupert Merson's entertaining, informative and up-to-date guide is intended for both the entrepreneur and the potential finance director. Straightforward and practical, it is the essential introduction to the subject.

ISBN 1 86197 454 X

£6.99

Non-executive Directors
A BDO Stoy Hayward Guide for Growing Businesses
by Rupert Merson

The role of the non-executive director has never before come under such scrutiny. From once being seen as 'about as useful as Christmas tree decorations', non-executives are now seen as critical components in the corporate governance framework, and important contributors to the strategic health of companies.

Rupert Merson explores the particular contribution the non-executive can make in the younger, growing, owner-managed business.

ISBN 1 86197 499 X

£6.99

Managing Directors
A BDO Stoy Hayward Guide for Growing Businesses
by Rupert Merson

Part inventor, part entrepreneur, part manager, part accountant, part leader, part salesman, part bottle-washer – the role
of managing director in the younger, growing business is one
of the most demanding jobs in commerce today. Yet it is sur-
prisingly little written about. Rupert Merson plugs the gap
with another of his insightful, irreverent, but as always informative guides.

ISBN 1 86197 740 9

£6.99

Owners
A BDO Stoy Hayward Guide for Growing Businesses
by Rupert Merson

The three key barriers to growth in any business with ambitions to grow are easy to identify: owners, owner-managers and managers. More's the pity that owners at least are little written about and less understood. Rupert Merson, in the fourth in his series on the key roles at the top of the growing business, explores perhaps the most important role of all.

ISBN 1 86197 682 8

£6.99

An Inspector Returns
The A–Z to surviving a tax investigation
by Daniel Dover & Tim Hindle
with cartoons by Michael Heath

Revised and updated second edition

If you are the subject of a tax investigation by the HMRC, do not panic – read this book instead. An investigation undoubtedly means trouble, but the straightforward advice in these pages should help steer you around the worst pitfalls and survive the process intact.

'An amusing guide through this difficult subject … This disarmingly honest little book could save you many sleepless nights.' *The Times*

ISBN 1 86197 420 5

£6.99

War or Peace
Skirmishes with the Revenue
by Daniel Dover & Tim Hindle
with cartoons by McLachlan

Each year over 250,000 people are subject to HMRC enquiries. It is not a pleasant experience. But help is at hand. For the first time here is a book that explains the whole process, along with numerous tips on how to proceed and what to do – or not to do. Deftly written with wit and humour, this could save you time, misery and money.

'This is a terrific book … It is informative, easy to understand and comforting. Full marks.' *The Tax Journal*

ISBN 1 86197 524 4

£6.99

Tax due on estate

Value of estate, £	Tax due, £	Effective tax rate, %
300,000	–	0
500,000	80,000	16
750,000	180,000	24
1,000,000	280,000	28
2,000,000	680,000	34
3,000,000	1,080,000	36

step is to consider your current capital position, and how much tax there might be on your estate. The next step is to write a will (see page 14), to ensure that you make the most of your nil-rate band and any other reliefs and exemptions that are available. Once you have done this, you might want to consider giving money away during your lifetime. Lifetime gifts are generally tax-free if they are made more than seven years before your death. This is covered in Chapter 3. However, before you consider lifetime giving you need to look at your current income and financial needs to decide what you can afford to give.

How much tax?

Before you can work out your likely IHT liability, you first have to calculate the current value of your estate. This involves drawing up a capital statement which is basically a valuation of all your assets and liabilities. The table on page 11 gives you an example of a capital statement.

As you can see from the example capital statement of Mr